THE ART OF BECOMING

Annabelle Gregory

A Memoir

The Art of Becoming

Annabelle Gregory

First published 2025 by Winter & Drew Publishing Ltd, Exeter.
Minor revision – March 2026.

Copyright © 2025-26 Annabelle Gregory. All rights reserved.

The right of Annabelle Gregory to be identified as the author of this work has been asserted by her in accordance with the Copyright, Designs and Patents Act 1988.

No part of this publication may be reproduced, stored in a retrieval system, or transmitted in any form or by any means, electronic, mechanical, photocopying, recording or otherwise, without the prior written permission of the publisher.

The author and publisher expressly prohibit the use of this work, in whole or in part, for the training, development, or improvement of artificial intelligence systems, large language models, machine learning algorithms, or any automated text generation or analysis systems, whether such use is direct or indirect.

Typeset in Garamond 12 point.

ISBN: 9781919208817

Also available as a Hardback and eBook.

The Art of Becoming

The story of a woman who has never stopped searching for beauty, never stopped creating, and even when life has tried to tell her otherwise, has never stopped becoming… herself.

The Art of Becoming is a candid, revealing, and irresistibly engaging memoir.

Annabelle proves that the most beautiful art is often the life that we choose to live.

Annabelle Gregory has dedicated her whole life to creating art. From life drawing to naive art to collaging, the breadth of her work is a reflection of her remarkable life journey.

The Art of Becoming
Annabelle Gregory
A Memoir

శుభ

Dedication

This memoir is dedicated to my children Marcus, Wayne and Sacha, and my grandchildren, Rosie, Lily, Robert and Richard.

Author's Note

The following memoir has been inspired by the people, places and events I have experienced throughout my eighty-four years. While I have tried to represent the situations and conversations as accurately as I can recall (or have researched from pictures, articles and the internet), I will admit to having used some creative licence here and there, especially where my memory is a little hazy – which it can be, particularly with something as specific as the date or location of an incident.

So I apologise if any scene or conversation is not exactly as others might have recalled, or if I have moved an incident in time or place, or if I have changed names (to protect identities) – but my intention has always been to bring the stories to life as I believe they *most likely* unfolded, based on the reality of what I know ultimately *did* happen.

Annabelle Gregory

Contents

Becoming A Floppy-Eared Rabbit 7
Becoming An Artist (And Critic) 13
Becoming A Writer 21
Becoming A Junior Naturalist 27
Becoming A Style Icon In Ballet Flats 39
Becoming A Ton-Up Girl 49
Becoming A Model (Part 1) 55
Becoming Part Of The Soho Coffee Culture 65
Becoming a Jet-Setter 71
Becoming A Model (Part 2) 81
Becoming A Model (Part 3) 89
Becoming Mrs Gregory 97
Becoming The Face of So Many Brands 107
Becoming The Boss's Wife 115
Becoming A Mother 123
Becoming The Girl About Town 129
Becoming A Target Of The Vice Squad 139
Becoming Madeline From M&S 149
Becoming Relaxed – The Calm Before The Storm 159
Becoming Stronger 169
Becoming an Artist Again 177
Becoming a Collage Artist, and a Hearse Driver 183
Becoming an Understanding Mother 197
Becoming Intrigued By My Son's Resourcefulness 205
Becoming The Cause Of A Teenage Tantrum 211
Becoming A Hospital Mother 217
Becoming A Weekend Antique Dealer 227
Becoming A Life Class Teacher 235
Becoming At Home In Devon 247
Becoming the Heart And Soul 255
Becoming Reconciled With Mother 267
Becoming A St Ives Artist 273
Becoming A Widow 285
And finally – Becoming Annabelle Gregory 291
Acknowledgements 296

'Harvest Time'

**South Hams landscape, oil on canvas, unframed.
90cm x 71cm.**

I love the rolling hills and mellow colours of this view near Modbury and felt it needed to be captured. Using oils gave me the chance to add the necessary texture and depth to the painting.

This landscape has been hanging in my landing these past few years, so I see it every time I walk up the stairs. As I'm going to be describing my search for beauty in my art and photographs throughout this book, this seemed a great place to start!

Prologue

Becoming A Floppy-Eared Rabbit

I never wanted to be a floppy-eared rabbit.

Hold that thought.

From a very young age, I was fascinated by beautiful things. I was absorbed by beauty all around; the garden plants with the amazingly perfect structure of their leaves; the flowers on the Common that smelled divine; the tall, majestic trees that just demanded to be climbed; the birds that sang their arias outside my bedroom window. Even as a small girl I wanted to be surrounded by beauty.

So when there was a stage production at my infant school and the teacher informed me I was to appear in a rabbit costume, I knew there was little beauty in that.

No, eight-year-old Annabelle Sylvester was never going to demean herself by being a boring old rabbit. She was going to be something altogether more lovely.

So I went home and told my mother I was going to be a fairy. I would need a pretty dress.

"A fairy?" my mother repeated absently, focusing on the costume she was hunched over, drawing together a sequinned bodice and tulle skirt with the tiniest of stitches.

"What are you making?" I asked, running my hand across the thin material.

"It's for a girl at the Aida Foster Stage School," she replied, then looked up with a frown. "A fairy dress, Annabelle? Are you sure?"

I gave her my most earnest expression and nodded.

She went back to the stitching, her hands moving in quick, deft flicks. "I'll make you something," she said. "There'll be enough of this tulle left over after I've made all the costumes. I was planning on using it for one of the London Palladium panto ones." Her hands paused, and she glanced up. "But I'll find something else. You'll look very pretty, Annabelle." She paused. "Now, go and get your bread and jam."

Of course, the lie was inevitably discovered, as I should always have known it would be.

It was on one of those unexpected days when my mother came to school to pick me up. I saw her talking to the teacher as I skipped across the playground, swinging my satchel and preparing for my usual solitary walk home. I stumbled to a stop and stared aghast at the two of them, my mother with a puzzled frown and the teacher shaking her head. I knew from the sinking feeling in the pit of my stomach that my secret was out.

I could just imagine the conversation.

"How are you getting on with the rabbit costume for Annabelle?" asks the teacher.

"Rabbit?" my mother replies. "I wasn't told anything about a rabbit. She said a fairy costume. I've made her a dress. With a tulle skirt."

"But Annabelle is not playing a fairy; she's going to be a *rabbit...*"

That must have been the moment when my mother caught sight of me standing a few yards away, no doubt white-faced with horror as I considered running back into the school to hide. But I stood my ground as she strode over. "Why did you lie?" she asked, a look of cold disappointment on her face.

I felt a tear start down my cheek. "Sorry," I whispered.

"I made you a dress," she went on. "One for a ruddy fairy!"

"I don't want to be a silly old rabbit," I said with a sniff. "I want to be pretty."

"Well, that's too bad," Mother replied.

"But can I still wear it?"

"Certainly not."

And I never did. She hung it up on the wall just out of my reach, so I had to see it every day. It was a painful reminder – not only of the bare-faced lie I had told, but also of the sacrifice she had made by using the material meant for a Palladium costume.

Standing on the stage a week later, looking perfectly dreadful in my hastily knocked up rabbit costume (complete with a pair of floppy felt ears glued to an old Alice band), I made a vow to myself. It was something that has since become so deeply ingrained, such a well-defined part of my being, that even now, in my eighties, I can only thank the little girl in the floppy ears for having had the idea.

It was that I would never again be without beauty in my life, wherever and however I could find it.

With the benefit of hindsight, I can honestly say that this search for beauty has been the driving force throughout my life. It's as if that pretty dress hanging on the wall just out of my reach showed how beauty is always something to be strived for – and that I should never be satisfied until I've done my utmost to find it.

I think this is also at the heart of my lifelong need to create art – through paint and collage, and particularly life drawing. Is the human body the perfect expression of beauty? Perhaps. Or is it the delicate petals of a flower? Or even an exquisitely made dress?

Finding the answer to these questions has been a part of my life, and that is what I want to share with you in this memoir. There have been many ups and downs, but my art has usually been a constant, and many of the events in my life can be clearly associated with a piece that I created at the time. Or as a result. And at times when my life became so frenetic the art had to take a back seat – such as when I was a model appearing in magazines and on TV ads, or when my children were small – then there are photographs or artefacts that bring the events and people back into sharp focus.

It was this thought that recently sent me into my attic to rummage around in the many old boxes and portfolio cases gathering dust. These had been stacked up there when I first moved in, four years ago. As I went over to them, it was as if they had been waiting patiently for their chance to be rediscovered – to have their moment in the light once again.

Opening each box was like a journey into another part of my life. Memories came flooding back as I held each artwork, photo or artefact up to the single bulb. Suddenly the years fell away, and I was in Pimlico with my grandmother, snuggling up in the warm socks she had knitted specially for me. Or in London in the Swinging Sixties, living it up with my husband-to-be, Barry, before heading down to Saint-Tropez with his family. And back there again immediately after, to shoot an ad for Player's cigarettes with Cy Endfield.

Another picture and I'm in Barry's restaurant in Mayfair, helping to clear up after a destructive visit by the Kray twins.

Then I'm back in London, raising my family. Before a picture takes me out to Oxfordshire, when we moved there for a more peaceful life.

A photo comes out of the box, and I'm a teenager again in London, as my father set up his taxi firm. How could I have forgotten how he had to defend his turf in one of the first of the 'taxi wars' of the early 1960s?

So many pieces. So many memories.

It's a life in pictures; each one telling its own unique story. And each one taking me closer to finding the answer to the question set by the little girl on stage in her rabbit costume.

Is it possible to find the true meaning of beauty?

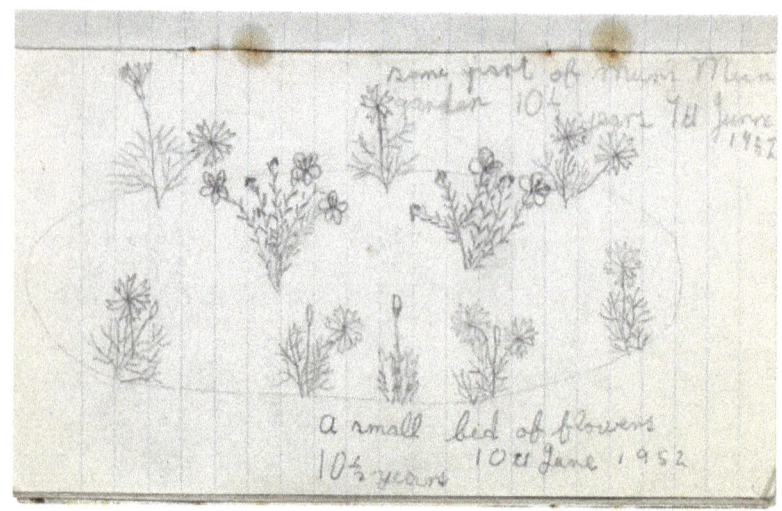

'A Small Bed of Flowers'

Pencil on lined notebook. 16.5cm x 9cm.

Coming across this notebook took me straight back to my earliest attempts at art. Even though it is clearly the work of a small girl, I remember being so proud of this drawing. Perhaps it was that pride that gave me the confidence to build and develop as an artist?

I suppose we all have to start somewhere!

Chapter One

Becoming An Artist (And Critic)

My great-grandfather painted dreadfully boring pictures.
 Enormous canvasses of Swiss lakes and mountains.
 Boring.
 They were in my grandmother Mum Mum's house when I was growing up. Hers was a rather stylish place – if such a thing was possible in Whyteleafe, near Croydon, in the early 1950s. It was next door to our own place, and the contrast could not have been more clear. Ours was a damp and mouldy little bungalow, complete with water dripping off the walls.

I visited my grandmother often – if only to get away from the mould – and couldn't help seeing these pictures in every room. It was as if she was trying to create some sort of alpine chalet, with each dull old picture pretending to be a window, despite being in large, ornate gold frames. The artist was Swiss, so I suppose he was just painting what he saw, but his ability to suck the beauty out of such glorious landscapes struck me, even as a child. I would stare at these pictures, my hands on my hips and my head to one side, as I tried to understand how such a beautiful subject could be rendered so lifeless. Was it the poor composition? The choice of colour? The heaviness of the brushwork?

Even then I knew enough to be a critic.

Perhaps it was those pictures that cemented my resolve to become an artist myself. It may be that art was in my blood – he was an ancestor after all – but it was the realisation that art could be done so badly that made me determined to do it better myself.

My grandmother found me one day when I was about ten and a half, staring at one of these paintings.

"You like it, ja, Annabelle?" she asked, in her thick German accent.

I didn't answer immediately. Back then I might not have been as plain-speaking as I am now, and she could be rather strict, so I considered my response carefully. "I think the trees on the side of the lake are what you're made to look at," I replied. "Not the mountains behind. Why is that? And the dull sky – it's awful. It's grey and it's flat, just like the rest of the picture."

As I say, I was quite the little critic.

"I see," she said with a slow frown. Then she gave me a slightly vague smile. "My father-in-law, he painted this. Perhaps you will be an artist like him?"

I looked up at her. "I want to be an artist," I said, "but not like that. I shall be better."

She seemed to let the slur on her father-in-law pass. "Then you must practice." A few days later, she surprised me with a blank lined notebook with a plain cover, plus a couple of pencils. "There," she said. "If you are to be an artist, you will need these."

"Oh, thanks!" I said, flicking through the blank pages and imagining what pictures I would put there. "I'm going to do lots of lovely drawings."

I was as good as my word, experimenting on every page. Nothing was safe from the attention of my pencil and paper; not flowers, plants, birds or trees – all were studied carefully and immortalised in the notebook. It was as if little Annabelle was fighting back against the tyranny of the ever-present Swiss mountain scenes; seeking to find the beauty in the natural world she believed these paintings so sadly lacked.

I came across this old notebook when I was rooting around in the attic. It was hiding amongst bits of junk in an old wooden box. I took it out carefully, and I will admit there was a small tear in my eye as I opened a random page. It was as if I was back in the orchard behind my grandparents' place, frowning as I studied a bed of wildflowers, my pencil poised and ready over the blank page. I remember wondering, as I knelt on the muddy grass, how to capture the beauty in their random hues and shapes. Then I leaned in until the flowers were the only thing I could see, their lovely rich scent making my head seem so full. The picture I drew seems very childish now, but I remember at the time how greatly it pleased me, and that was the important thing.

I don't recall ever showing my drawings to anyone else; not to my grandmother, my parents or even my younger sisters, Ingrid and Charlotte. I was a solitary child, very independent, and lived in my own little world. I was at one with nature, spending hours in the garden, the orchard or even the local common, enjoying the peace and solitude of my own company. It was a world of wonder and exploration; every leaf, every flower, every tree was studied with the greatest of care before committing their image to this notebook, as well as its many successors.

Looking back, I do wonder now whether I was a free spirit because my family left me to myself, or whether my family did this precisely because I was clearly so much happier on my own. Whichever it was, the net result was that my parents were quite content to let me get on with my life – while they mollycoddled and spoiled my little sisters. Even though I was the eldest, I was the one who got the hand-me-downs. As an experienced seamstress, my mother would shorten and take in her own dresses, then present them as if she was doing me a massive favour.

"Why can't I have anything new?" I asked one day, as she was kneeling down and measuring the hem of an old utility dress she had made me try on. "Clothes rationing is finished now." This was in the summer of 1952, not long after my grandmother had given me the notebook.

"Because 'make do and mend' is more responsible," she muttered through the pins clamped between her teeth. "And we don't have money to throw around." This was true. My father, a conscientious objector in the war (who would hide in wardrobes to avoid the draft), used to catch rabbits for us to eat.

"But Ingrid gets new dresses," I observed, trying not to sound too bitter. "You made her that new white one, and she insists on pirouetting around with her hands above her head." I gave a dismissive snort. "She said she was being Margot Fonteyn."

"She's a lot smaller than you. There's less fabric needed to make her something, and I could never alter one of my dresses to fit her."

"What about mine? She could have those when I'm too big for them."

Mother stood up and looked me squarely in the eye. "By the time you've ripped them on thorns or snagged them on the trees you climb, young lady, they're only good to be torn up for dishcloths." I must have looked surprised, as she put her hands on her hips and gave me a look of triumph. "Oh yes, I've seen you, high up in the branches of the oak tree behind Mother's house, sitting there like a little crow. It's a wonder you haven't fallen off and killed yourself by now." She gave a small sniff. "And I could hardly get the grass stains out of that skirt you wore last week," she added. "What were you doing?"

I recalled kneeling to study the wildflowers. "Drawing," I muttered.

"Can't you draw without getting mud and grass all over your clothes?"

I decided to change the subject. "It's not fair," I said. "I want something new. Something pretty. You make all those costumes for the girls at the London Palladium, and for the stage school. But you don't make one for your oldest daughter."

I glanced inadvertently up to where the fairy dress had hung for months after I'd lied about being a rabbit in the school production. Mother didn't say anything. She didn't need to; the only time she had made me a new dress, it was because I'd told her a fib.

Of course, I should never have told such an untruth, and in my defence, I had been quite small then. But even by this time, it seemed to have left my mother with a certain amount of scepticism about anything I told her.

This was aptly demonstrated by the episode of Mrs Lyons's ghost.

Let me explain.

Mrs Lyons was the old lady who had lived in the bungalow before us, and my grandmother informed me one day that Mrs Lyons had died in the house.

"She was in the back room – the bedroom for you and Ingrid."

"And she died there?" I asked, horrified by the idea of an old woman breathing her last in my very own bedroom, even if it was before we moved in.

"Ja ja." Mum Mum shrugged. "This happens."

"What did she die of?"

"She was very old," was all Mum Mum said, as if that was explanation enough.

I thought a moment. How could someone be so old they had to die? As a child, it seemed inconceivable one could get to such an age. The more I considered it, the more it played on my mind. Mrs Lyons started to assume an air of malevolence, as if her spirit could hardly bear the thought of two small girls sleeping in the room where she had died. Would she try and make us leave? Or maybe she already had; causing the walls to be so damp and mouldy that we'd have to go somewhere else... In my mind, Mrs Lyons became something of a monster, growing and swelling from a little old lady into a dreadful witch-like demon.

Then one evening, I actually saw her.

It was as I was lying in bed trying to sleep, that she came to the window. I stared in horror at the face outside. It was heavily wrinkled, with a large hooked nose, thin lips and hooded, piercing red eyes that seemed to see right through me. For a moment I was too frozen in fear to move or shout, but then the face slowly turned away. Now it seemed to be studying Ingrid, asleep in the other bed.

I found my voice. "Help!" I yelled. "Help! It's a ghost! It's Mrs Lyons!"

At this, the face turned back to me and gave a frown. It seemed to grow larger, so it almost filled the whole window.

I screamed.

A moment later, Mother ran in.

"What is it, Annabelle?"

I pointed breathlessly at the window. "Mrs... Mrs Lyons..." I managed in a strangled whisper. "A ghost!"

Mother glanced over to the window, then back at me. "There's nothing there," she snapped. "You've just had a bad dream, Annabelle. Go back to sleep."

Mrs Lyons gave me a slow, evil smile, as if she'd made her point. Then she faded away and disappeared.

"But I saw her!" I wailed, clutching my knees to my chest, as if to protect myself in case Mrs Lyons returned. "She was right there! Now she's gone!"

Mother came up beside me and put her hand on my forehead. "No fever," she muttered. "If anything, a little cold.

Go back to sleep, Annabelle, and stop your fibbing. Good little girls don't tell lies."

"I don't tell lies," I said. "I saw her."

"Leave it," she said. "Now, goodnight." Then she left the room.

I don't know what upset me the most – Mrs Lyons scaring me from outside my window, or Mother not believing me.

Looking back, I think it was the latter. Whether or not I dreamed it is not the point here; it's the feeling that my family never understood me. That they didn't believe me, even after I had learned my lesson from the rabbit costume incident. Maybe this made me even more determined to do my own thing; to make my own way in life.

To be forever a free spirit and pursue my search for the beauty of art.

'Standing Nude'

Life drawing, charcoal and pastel on paper, mounted and framed.

This was a picture that I originally hung in Bistro 35, Modbury, Devon. I put it up in my home when I retired – and it constantly reminds me of what fun we had in the Bistro.

Chapter Two

Becoming A Writer

I have introduced you to me as a child, but now I would like to step back for a moment and explain a bit more about why I am writing this memoir. And why my art – specifically life drawing – is so important.

A good starting point for this is Bistro 35, the bar/restaurant that my husband Barry and I owned and ran in Modbury, Devon. I'll talk in more detail in later chapters on how we came to be its proprietors and how, after running various clubs and restaurants in London, it came to be such a massive part of our lives – from 1999 until I closed it in 2022.

The Bistro, as it was simply known, was a cosy place; a home-from-home for the regulars and, I believe, an unexpected find for tourists. It was also a training-ground for the young people of Modbury; over the years we were there, Barry and I gave around thirty of the local kids employment, either in the kitchens or as waiting staff, teaching them not only the basics of hospitality and catering, but also the life skills of hard work and dedication. I am pleased to say that the Bistro Alumni are a great bunch, and even though they are now dispersed all around the world, I still keep in touch with as many of them as I can.

The Bistro furniture was deliberately chosen to be eclectic (the bar was an old altar – a great talking point), and the boldly coloured walls were covered in my art, some of which demonstrated my lifelong passion for life drawing. This, incidentally, prompted the following – somewhat disparaging – comment on a well-known travel review site: *"Went to the wine bar that forms part of the bistro for a drink, there appeared to be some sort of exhibition of naked drawings on."* The implied criticism (along with the low star rating) suggests this person was not impressed. Which only goes to show – when it comes to art, you can't please everyone.

We did have a loyal group of local regulars who seemed quite happy with the decor. Known as the 'Bistro Gang', they would come in for themed events such as the winter 'Film Nights', 'Bangers and Mash Wednesdays', and 'Cocktail of the Week'. Or they would just drop in at any time, simply for a relaxing drink and a chat with friends. I suspect that the art on the walls was all part of the homely atmosphere we tried to create for them, and, to a large degree, I think we succeeded.

Having said that, there's nothing like a drawing of a naked body to start a conversation.

When we first opened the Bistro, I was 'Front of House', while Barry was in the kitchen. He did the cooking; I did the meeting and greeting. I also served behind the bar. It was well known that Annabelle was a good listener; you could always get a sympathetic ear if you poured out your woes while she poured out the drinks. This was as true of the Bistro Gang as it was for the tourists – I found myself becoming everyone's agony aunt.

When Barry died, I kept the Bistro going for a few years, but now I have sold it, I find I have time for myself. I use the time to read – particularly biographies. This has made me realise that everyone else has interesting life stories; now it's time to tell my own. I think mine is just as interesting as the biographies I read; it's a life filled with love, loss, family, nature and many changes of scene. One driven by my art and my search for the beauty of the world.

And now that I can tell my story, I'm jolly well going to.

Writing a memoir is a cathartic process. It's an opportunity to 'get it all out there' – now that it's me who is the one 'propping up the bar' and pouring out their tale. I even have the old altar in my studio conservatory at home, so I can lean on it and tell my stories to the many friends and family who come round for tea, cake and a chat. Incidentally, it also reminds me of another eclectic bar; the one Barry had when he ran the Lords Club in London, which was a series of old upright pianos pushed together. But more of that later.

When it comes to me telling my story, life drawing has played a major part. The pictures I hung on the Bistro walls were only a small part of my overall body of work, and now it's my turn to talk, I want to explain why that is.

Throughout my years, art has meant many things to me – sketching nature, painting, collage – but life drawing has always been my first love. It's something I have never been able to get away from – nor have I wanted to.

What are the reasons for this?

Firstly, I find it liberating. I grew up in the 1950s, when a young lady was expected to display modesty and decorum. As a free-spirited child who became an independent young woman, I sought inspiration outside of these strict social bounds. I found that exploring and appreciating the natural beauty of the human body gave me the freedom I was looking for. This is why I have attended a life class whenever possible, and continue to do so, even into my eighties.

Secondly, it makes me appreciate stillness and mindfulness. In a life that has, at times, been quite frenetic, the act of slowing down, sitting still and drawing makes the fast-moving world outside seem to fade away. There is nothing but you, the model and the paper – and for that hour or two, the stresses and strains of life are on hold. It is always a magical time for me, and the number of life drawings I have done bears testament to that.

Finally, it's a chance to connect with another human being in a deeply personal way. They place their trust in you by posing; you must repay that trust by representing them with honesty and integrity. That means you have to pay attention to their form and understand it completely. You need to see it not just as a body, but as something made up of separate shapes and curves, of areas of light and shadow. Only then can you do justice to the beauty inherent in every human by turning them into a work of art. And, being a model is more than just the ability to stand still; it's a skill in its own right. I learned that from a lady called Susan at the Camden School of Art and I've never forgotten it. As the artist, one has a duty to the model to do them justice.

I have included one of my life pictures at the beginning of this chapter to illustrate my point. It was done at the Harbour House life class in Kingsbridge, Devon and was drawn in ten minutes. I was keen to capture the model's inner beauty – even from behind.

Now, back to my story. Read on for how I locked my art teacher in the supplies cupboard at my girls' grammar school, and when I started down the artist's path by enrolling at the St Martin's School of Art, even though my mother decided that was not a good thing. All steps on my journey to becoming the kind of artist I am today; one who can fill the walls of a bistro with drawings of naked bodies. Even if it prompts tourists to leave a poor review.

As I say, when it comes to art, you can't please everyone.

'Portrait of a Model'

Pencil on paper. 54cm x 39cm.

This portrait is of an eccentric old lady who used to wander up and down the street in a ballet tutu and was much in demand as a model. Finding this sketch reminded me of her eccentricity – which took me on to some of the other strange people in my life – such as my Nan with her pink statues, Miss Chown the art teacher and Miss Palmer, of the Junior Naturalist Club.

Chapter Three

Becoming A Junior Naturalist

If you want to excel at art, then it's a good idea to go to art school. So at the age of sixteen, I enrolled on a Foundation course at St Martin's in Charing Cross, London.

The journey that led me to such a prestigious place of learning (although I was not there for long – more of that later), was made up of a number of steps; each of which made me more and more sure that the world of art was the one for me.

I'd like to take you through these steps now, so you can understand why I came to that conclusion. On the way, I'll share with you the story of my father shooting a man in the stomach with arrows and burying him in sand. We'll find out what happened when my friend and I locked the art teacher at our grammar school in that cupboard; and we'll meet the amazing Miss Palmer at the Natural History Museum. Finally, we'll head off to Alderney on a nature trip.

Let's start with the first of these – the bizarre conjuring trick. My father's name was Tom Sylvester, and in my early life, he and my grandfather ran Sylvester's Three Ring Circus. At the time, it was the biggest circus of its type in England, touring the country from its base in Blackpool. This incident was when the circus was in the Dreamland theme park in Margate, and we were renting a house nearby. I must have been around seven or eight years old. My father wanted to do a trick he'd set up with one of the men in the circus (I have forgotten his name – it might have been one of the Kayes brothers, Johnny and Jimmy, who used to perform horse riding tricks in the ring). This 'stooge' was wearing a one-piece 'strongman' leotard, standing with his arms folded, looking as if he had not a care in the world. He was on the other side of the ring in front of a trench dug in the sand, while my father drew in the crowd.

"Roll up, roll up!" he called as people took their seats. "See the greatest escape act since Mr Houdini!" He glared around the crowd, as if challenging them to deny this was what he was about to deliver. Then he was handed a bow and a couple of arrows and fitted one to the bow.

"Not only will I shoot this man with an arrow, but I will bury his body under several feet of sand!" Again he looked around the crowd. "And then..." He gave a significant pause. "You will see with your very own eyes a miraculous escape!" He drew back the bow, aiming squarely at the stooge's belly. Then, just as the crowd (and me at the front) were taking an expectant gasp, he lowered the bow again. "Does anyone here think this cannot be done?" he asked. There was silence from the crowd, who were all staring wide-eyed at him. My father raised the bow once more. "Very well," he called out, "then let us see!"

My breath caught in my throat as I watched him draw back the bow, then release it with a loud 'twang'.

The arrow hit the man in his stomach, making him stagger, but he did not fall. My father fitted another arrow and shot the man again. This time, the man staggered backwards, the two arrows protruding from his belly, and fell into the trench. Immediately two stagehands ran forward with shovels and covered the stooge with sand.

There was an excited murmur from the crowd as the sand was shovelled up to the top of the trench, then the stagehands brought a small tent over, and dropped it onto the spot. With the tent in place, all eyes turned back to my father. "Now!" he shouted as he held their attention; a twinkle in his eye I recognised well. "How long do you think a man can survive after being shot with two arrows and buried under sand?"

There were calls of "a minute!", "two!", and my father acknowledged these with another smile and a small wave of his hand.

"Indeed," he observed, seeming to know he held the crowd's undivided attention. "Then let us see how long before he escapes!" A drum roll started just as he said this, building to a crescendo. Then, to a gasp from the crowd, the flap of the tent was pulled back, and the man in the leotard stepped out. There were no arrows in his belly, and he seemed to be perfectly hale and hearty, staring around the ring, acknowledging the applause of the crowd.

Why am I telling you this? Not because it led directly to St Martin's, but because it showed the kind of man my father was – "all show and no blow," as my German grandmother once said. And because it brought my father to the attention of the authorities in Margate (I believe the Daily Mirror ran the story), which meant the landlord of our apartment decided to demand the rent that my father seemed to have 'forgotten' to pay.

As a result, we had to leave the flat – and Margate – very quickly one night, and this led us to London, where the next stage of my story takes place.

While my grandfather took the circus back up to Blackpool, my mother, father, my sisters and I arrived in London in a state of total penury. We were homeless, which meant we were put into some dreadful 'halfway house' full of screaming children. After our rented flat in Margate, which had been reasonably warm, dry and quiet, I found the whole thing quite bewildering. I do recall coming in one day from playing in the street, to find my parents having a blazing row; my mother standing in the middle of the room with her hands on her hips, glaring at my father, who seemed to be trying to burrow his way backwards into a threadbare old armchair.

"We're better than this!" my mother was screaming. "How am I supposed to bring up three little girls in this squalor?" She waved her hand around the dingy room, with its peeling brown wallpaper, smoke-stained ceiling and rickety utility furniture. "So what are you going to do about it?"

My father seemed cowed into silence at that moment, but a few days after, a solution was found – and I have to say it was an unusual one.

The family was split up.

As my father pointed out, if bringing up three girls in such squalor wasn't possible, then something had to give way – and what he gave away was... me and Ingrid.

While my mother, father and littlest sister Charlotte stayed together in the poky room, I was dispatched to live with my Nan, my father's mother, in her large, shabby flat in Tachbrook Street, Pimlico. Ingrid went to stay with our aunt (my father's sister), in a prefab in the Vauxhall Bridge Road.

I found my Nan's place to be dull; painted in a uniform, drab, wartime brown, which immediately lowered my spirits even further. But I soon realised that this first impression was wide of the mark; Nan was a lovely person who looked after me very well. The same, however, cannot be said of the school I was sent to. It was called St James the Less – which stood for 'less good' in my opinion. It was an all-girls' primary with no heating, while learning consisted of repeating our times-tables every day by rote. We also had needlework classes where we made aprons, and had to do exactly thirty-five stitches to an inch. Very Victorian!

One bright spot in all the drabness was when my name was drawn out of a hat to go in a group to the Embankment and see the coronation of the new Queen. I'll never forget the brief glimpse we had of the magnificent coach with beautiful young

Queen Elizabeth inside. We screamed with excitement as it emerged from the grey rain like a golden fairy-tale vision. I would love to have been able to draw it, but it flashed past all too quickly. I suppose today all the kids would have photographed it on their phones, but in those days, you needed a camera – not something I possessed.

Nan was what we would now call 'somewhat eccentric'. She had a pair of large plaster statues of pink ladies either side of the mantelpiece, and she would paint them with another coat of pink paint at least once a year. I suppose eventually there was more paint on them than plaster.

I used to go out and explore the local market and high street, and was particularly fascinated by the man who offered a service darning ladders in stockings, which he did in the window of his shop. I used to stare for what seemed like hours as he made careful stitches to repair the stockings. 'Make do and mend' was still very much alive back then; and not something I suppose you'd find in today's more throwaway society.

Although I enjoyed my time with Nan, eventually the family came back together again.

We were given a council flat at a new development called De Quincy House, heated by the water coming from Battersea Power Station. Now we were living in such luxury, my mother's natural snobbery reappeared, and she decided the secondary modern school nearby was simply not good enough. No, her little Annabelle was not going to rough it there, she would be going to the local grammar school. Which meant I had to pass the entrance exam – the Eleven Plus.

Unfortunately, St James the Less had lived up to its name, and I had been woefully unprepared for the exam. I failed it miserably. But that was not going to stop Mother. Once she had decided I was going, a small thing like failing the entrance exam was a minor detail.

I later found out that she had marched into the headmistress, Miss Ewart's, office, with the school secretary virtually trying to pull her out again, planted her hands on the desk, leaned forward and told poor Miss Ewart that I must be accepted.

"My daughter is an incredibly talented drawer and seamstress," she apparently barked. "She deserves a place!"

"I'm sorry, but she has failed..." Miss Ewart began.

"The failure here is not by Annabelle!" Mother interrupted. "It is by the appalling primary school, who have done nothing to bring out her natural abilities."

"That's as may be, but..."

"But!" Mother repeated, and I can imagine the steely look in her eye. "If they had done their job, then we wouldn't be having this conversation! She would already have a place."

"Well, I can understand you are upset, Mrs Sylvester, but..."

"Don't you keep 'butting' me, Miss Ewart!" I suspect at this point my mother wagged her finger in the poor headmistress's face. "It is your job to give the best education to girls who qualify, and not only is Annabelle perfectly capable, she would have shown it if that school had prepared her correctly."

At some point Miss Ewart must have bowed to the inevitable and conceded. I was admitted to the Carlyle Grammar School for Girls, resplendent in the uniform made for me by my mother.

I had a great time at Carlyle and made lots of friends; but there was one (slightly shameful) episode when I was probably around thirteen, which I will share because it moved me on to the next part of my journey towards art school.

The episode involved the art teacher, Miss Chown; a decrepit old dear with buck teeth. I'm not proud, but on one occasion, my friend Joan and I thought it would be great fun if we locked her in the art cupboard. She had gone in to fetch some pencils and left the key in the door. As soon as she went inside, we ran up, shut the door, and turned the key. Then we ran off, giggling at our daring. But then we started to feel remorse, at the thought of the kindly teacher sitting all alone in the cupboard.

"We have to let her out," I said to Joan.

"She'll be cross," Joan replied, with a slightly superior look.

"The longer we leave her, the more cross she'll be," I pointed out.

There was a pause as Joan considered this. "We'll unlock the door and run," she suggested. "Then she won't know it was us."

But Miss Chown knew exactly who the culprits were and made us both stay behind after class. As she sat us down, Joan and I gave each other a nervous glance; this was going to be a stern ticking off. But we could not have been more wrong.

Miss Chown gave us a toothy smile and said, "Now girls, I know that was a bit of fun for you both, but it was not a particularly happy experience for me." She paused, then said, "While I was locked in, I was thinking what I should do about it."

Joan and I shared another glance. Where was this going?

"I have decided that as a consequence, you will do an assignment for me." Another pause. "I want you to visit a museum and do some drawings. I want to see at least three different sketches from you both, and I shall expect them to be the best you can do. I suggest the Natural History Museum in South Kensington."

Which is why, a few days later, Joan and I came to be standing in the main hall of the museum, staring up at the massive diplodocus skeleton (which I believe is affectionately known as 'Dippy'), towering over us. Naturally, this was the first drawing we each did for Miss Chown, before moving on to explore further.

I came across the skeleton of a giant sea turtle, so this was my second drawing.

It was while I was later absorbed in my third drawing – a large fern with incredibly intricate leaves – that a woman bounded up to me and peered down at my pad.

"Oh my!" came a breathy voice. "You have a real talent, young lady!"

I looked up to see an absolute vision of chic.

From the red beret at a jaunty angle over her peroxide blonde hair, to the blue pin-up dress with large white polka dots, to the high-heeled sling-backs, this woman had it all. I had never seen such a person, and I suspect I just stared at her open-mouthed. She pointed down at my drawing.

"You have really captured the way that frond curls," she said. "It's not easy, but you've managed to get it." She held a hand out for the pad. "Can I have a closer look?"

As I handed it over, I noticed a gaggle of girls of roughly my own age standing behind this vision, all carrying sketchpads of their own. They were watching our exchange with interest.

"Really very good," the woman said, handing it back. She gave me a big smile. "Miss Palmer," she announced.

I took it this was her introduction. "Annabelle Sylvester," I replied.

"Well, Annabelle," she said, "I think you show great promise as an artist." She gestured at the gaggle of girls. "I run the Junior Naturalist Club. It's a group that helps young people develop their art, and particularly their nature drawing. We have a trip coming up to one of the Channel Islands, Alderney. I would love for you to join us." She gave me an even bigger smile, as if she was the sun shining bright. "Will you come?"

My mother was less than impressed when I got home and announced that I was going on a nature trip to Alderney.

"Who is going to pay for this?" she demanded.

"Miss Palmer says the club will," I answered, putting my hands on my hips for emphasis. "She runs the Junior Naturalist Club. Her father was a captain in the war, and he provides all the money. Anyway, it's going to be fun. I will learn about botany. And it's an island. I've never been to an island before."

"Do you know any of these people?" she asked.

"I spoke to them at the museum," I said. "The girls are all very nice." They had certainly been welcoming, and I had got to know a couple of them before we had finally parted, the ebullient Miss Palmer leading them away.

Finally, after some huffing and puffing, Mother agreed, and I went on the trip.

Alderney was beautiful; something I appreciated more and more as we ventured out each day from the nunnery where we were staying, studying and drawing the landscape and plants.

Not only was it a wonderful experience, but the beginning of a life-long love of the island that has brought me – and my family – back many times. I see it as one of the first 'key to freedom' moments, that established art as the driving force in my life, and led me to taking the Foundation course at St Martin's School of Art.

In the next chapter I will take you to that prestigious school; a place I did not attend for long, but which had a profound effect on my future.

'Waterloo Autos'

Pen and ink on paper. 37cm x 27cm.

Of all the art I did in my time at St Martin's, this is the only one I seem to have kept. It's as much a reminder of a nearly disastrous incident with a car-dealer, as it is a study in technical drawing and perspective.

Chapter Four

Becoming A Style Icon In Ballet Flats

My mother had got me into Carlyle, but I got myself into St Martin's.

It was Miss Chown who took me to one side and told me this should be my next step.

"You have to develop your art, my dear," she said, making me stay behind one day after class. "Those drawings you did at the Natural History Museum, and the ones you showed me from Alderney – they make it clear you have a real talent. You must do a Foundation course at an art college, so you can then decide what discipline to specialise in." She gave me a significant stare. "And, of course, you can't do better than St Martin's School of Art in the Charing Cross Road. Work like yours is what they look for in a student."

I thought from that she meant I simply had to show them my work, and I'd be in. Which is why I caught the bus to the Charing Cross Road shortly after, clutching my portfolio of drawings, determined to secure a place for the term after I left Carlyle.

I was sixteen years old and did not have the first idea about applying correctly; I was simply taking Miss Chown at what I thought was her word. I assumed that if I turned up, they would be bound to let me in.

But even then, I wasn't leaving anything to chance. I not only had to show my talents, I had to impress the St Martin's people with what I fondly imagined was a suitably bohemian-artist style. I dressed carefully that morning, choosing a sweater dress and a Miss Palmer-inspired beret on top of my shoulder-length hair. The dress was really very short, so I pulled on a pair of sheer black tights, then observed the whole effect in the mirror. My legs looked a bit too daring, so another pair went on over the top. Finally, I finished off the whole ensemble with some yellow ballet flats.

As I studied my reflection, I turned to each side, putting my hand on my chin in a thoughtful pose, pouting in what I fondly thought was a provocative way. I'd been following the top models of the day, especially those like Leila Williams and Jean Crook who'd reached the finals of Miss Great Britain, as well as new up-and-coming models such as Jean Shrimpton. I'd been fascinated by seeing them posing for the cameras on the cinema newsreels and in the magazines.

As I stood in front of the mirror, I was one of these models. In my head I was hearing the clicks and whirrs of the photographer's camera as it captured my every move, to the shouts of "Now, look to your left, Annabelle! That's it! Give me sultry! Give me sexy! Great pose, Annabelle! Great pose! That's it, that's the one! That's the shot!" Then the final, "And... relax! Great work, Annabelle. Great work. Beautiful! You are beautiful!"

This vision of modelling style turned up outside the St Martin's building and stopped in the street to gather herself before pushing through the doors. There was probably a lot of noise, but I don't really remember – maybe some drilling and hammering, as there was much post-war re-building going on at the time, and I suppose, the clatter of cars, cabs and busses on the Charing Cross Road. But none of these made a great impression on me. No, my attention was all on the Victorian-looking building with large windows and a sign with a shield proclaiming it as the *St Martin's School of Art*.

As I stood, students started spilling out into the street; young men in tailored jackets and jeans, while the girls were in either sweater dresses like mine, tight-fitting pencil skirts, or even a few in full A-line skirts with pinched-in waists. They were carrying sketchbooks, canvas rolls or art bags, and all looked very intense; no doubt discussing weighty topics of art, fashion, design and culture as they came down the steps and walked away. The street was full of small shops selling things like clothes, books and food, and as they disappeared into these shops, I felt a deep yearning to become a student like them. Yes, being a model would be great, but first, I wanted to study art and fashion. I had it all worked out.

Emboldened by this thought, I marched up the steps, dodged past a couple more students, and went inside.

The lobby was cool and peaceful, with a desk in one corner. Behind it was an older woman wearing winged glasses. She had heavily set hair, and a scowl on her face that put me in mind of a bulldog.

"I want to see someone from Admissions, please," I announced.

The bulldog woman looked down her nose. "Do you have the name of the person you're seeing?" she enquired. "Or even an interview appointment?" This gave me only a small pause; if my mother could win over Miss Ewart, who was rather tall and quite fearsome to us girls, then getting past this gatekeeper should be easy.

"No," I replied, with what I hoped was a winning smile and an engaging tilt of my head, "but I have a portfolio." I paused, as her face remained impassive. I half expected her to lift one side of her mouth and growl. "And I have a recommendation from my art teacher, Miss Chown," I persevered, "from the Carlyle Grammar School for Girls." I put extra emphasis on the 'Grammar' just to make sure she got the point. "I'm sure you've heard of her?"

"Not at all," the woman said, with a sneer that actually did lift one side of her mouth. "If you don't have an app—"

"Miss Chown?" said a voice behind me, cutting off the bulldog woman.

I turned to see a tall man in a tweed jacket with dark, wavy hair and a slight smile. "I once met an art teacher called Miss Chown." He tapped on his mouth. "Teeth like an old rabbit, if I remember rightly."

"Yes," I said breathlessly. "That's her." I did feel a small pang of guilt that we were using such a personal feature to identify my teacher, but if it could get me in, then I was sure she'd understand.

"Frank Martin, Head of Sculpture," he said, holding out his hand.

"Annabelle Sylvester," I replied as I shook it.

"And you've come to apply for the Foundation course?" he asked. I nodded. "All right then," he said, "come with me and let's take a look at your work."

As I followed him across the lobby, I swear I heard a growl from behind.

❧

I rushed home on a high of excitement; Mr Martin had been so impressed with my portfolio that he had accepted me onto the next Foundation course on the spot. I know now that this was highly unusual, but at the time I thought this was how these things worked.

Sadly, my mother seemed unwilling to share in my success.

"You just turned up?" she gasped. "Like... like... that?" She paused, standing back with her hands on her hips and a look on her face like she'd just smelled a rotten egg. "In a dress that barely covers you, and..." she frowned as she peered at my legs, "is that two pairs of tights? And those shoes! What were you thinking?"

"It's what they all wear," I said, adding a touch of defiance to my voice. "I saw girls coming out and there were some dressed just like this. It's the latest look."

"Well, I didn't get you into a good school like Carlyle so you could go around looking like a French tart. Why can't you go to a secretarial school? No man's going to want you if you're a penniless artist. You'll need to get a good job and earn money. Artists don't earn anything."

It was at this point that the last remnants of my bubble burst, leaving me feeling quite empty, and perhaps even a little sick. How naïve to think she would be pleased for me!

At the time I was desperately upset, but now I look back, I can see why she didn't like the idea of me dressing bohemian and going to art school. Money was as tight as ever, and I suppose she wanted me to start contributing. She had recently set up her own dress shop called Welti's (her German maiden name), and I know she was struggling to make an income from it. She had previously been bringing private clients to our flat in De Quincy House for dress fittings, but it had been difficult, as one of the local residents had been using the lifts as a urinal. Mother had to bleach it to get rid of the smell before any clients came to the flat. Setting up her own shop meant she didn't have to worry about that any more, but instead, she had all the costs of the premises to consider.

I suppose, as a high-end dressmaker, she didn't want her own daughter looking like – as she put it – a 'French tart'!

Meanwhile Father was now running a fleet of mini-cab taxis in the West End – so he was working all hours and struggling to bring in the money. I'll go into more on this in a later chapter.

But – however upset I might have been with Mother – I wasn't going to back down. I had got myself into St Martin's, and I was jolly well going. So in September, around the time of my seventeenth birthday, I began my Foundation course.

A typical day at St Martin's would include life drawing – and gave me my first experience of a male body (although their most private parts were tucked into a buff-coloured pouch). Mother was suitably unimpressed. "Oh, they teach that do they?" she asked with an arched eyebrow when I first showed her my work. "All these men getting their clothes off in front of young girls..." her disapproval hung in the air, until I showed her another drawing, this time of a woman in her sixties wearing nothing but a tutu and ballet shoes. "Most odd," was her only comment. But I loved the discipline of daily life drawing, and have never lost my enjoyment of it to this day.

Our tutors were a remarkable bunch. Joe Tilson – an earnest dark-haired man with thick-rimmed glasses and a cigarette always in hand – introduced us to pop art, while Eduardo Paolozzi would lecture us in his gruff accent that was part Scottish and part Italian about how art comes from anywhere, even junk. To prove it he would show us sculptures he'd made with bits of old metal he'd reclaimed from a breaker's yard. Elizabeth Frink taught us how to subvert the traditions of sculpture. Instead of chiselling material away to make a piece, she would add plaster to an armature and work it up to create a rough, almost formless surface. This defined her style, and to this day, I use her subversion of form and building up of material in my own work: particularly in my paper collages.

My friend Annie and I would go out with our sketchbooks, as we were supposed to draw buildings in order to better understand architectural form. Annie was a girl of my own age, a pretty blonde with a snub nose and brown eyes. We had started going round together after being put next to each other in life drawing, and both trying to stifle a giggle when the first male model peeled off his trousers. I do recall one day when we saw a car sales garage, with a row of cars parked up in front of a dirty old caravan where the salesman sat. I nudged Annie. "Let's draw that," I said. She agreed, so we opened our stools and sat. After about half an hour, an old grey-haired chap in a flat cap and a dirty looking sheepskin coat came out of the caravan and walked over to us.

"What are you doing?" he asked with a leery grin. "Two pretty young girls like you?"

"We're from the art school," I said. "Doing a drawing. I hope you don't mind."

"Let me see," he said, coming round behind us and peering over our shoulders. His breath stank, and I leaned away as much as I could. "Very good," he said. Thankfully he moved round and stood in front of us. "I'd like to buy the pictures."

Annie and I glanced at each other. This was an unexpected bonus.

"Come into the caravan, girls, and we can talk." He gave another, even more leery grin.

I had a sudden vision of what might happen if we went in there with him, and said, "Sorry, no. We're not allowed to sell our work." I nudged Annie again. "Come on, we've got to get back."

We picked up our stools and fairly ran, leaving him standing in the road.

To this day, I can't watch an episode of *Minder* without wincing at the Arthur Daley character. Too similar to that old man.

Overall, my year at St Martin's was a happy one, and I was starting to think what I would specialise in, when it all came to a sudden, crashing end. Mother's disapproval had become even stronger as the year progressed, and she made it clear that I did not have the luxury of staying on for a degree course.

"Absolutely not," she said when I told her this was what I wanted. "You've had your fun for a year; but there's no future in an art education. Now it's time to get a job and start bringing in money."

Despite my protests, she was adamant. So I reluctantly left at the end of the year and got a job. And although I didn't get any further art education, I do know how much I learned. St Martin's set me up for a life in art, and I kept learning in different ways.

Oh, and one other thing; during that year, I met the man I was going to marry – Barry Gregory.

Article in Woman's Own, 28 February 1959

Before I met Barry Gregory, I had been seeing a lad called Joe Brooks. We got in *Woman's Own* because we epitomised the 'rebel look' of the Chelsea Set.

Photo courtesy of Future plc.

Chapter Five

Becoming A Ton-Up Girl

My husband Barry died on 2 May 2014.

That night I opened the Bistro as usual – mainly because I couldn't think of any good reason why I shouldn't. And because Barry would have expected it.

Some friends invited me round to their place for supper; I suppose to get me out of the bar for a couple of hours, while another friend stayed behind to keep it running.

But the Bistro pulled me back; almost as if by going in as usual, I was denying that Barry had truly gone. After a marriage lasting fifty-four years on and off (sometimes very off – more of that later), he had, indeed, gone.

I remember collapsing into the big armchair by the bar, while everyone from the Bistro Gang – Fiona, Graham and all the rest – fluttered around me, like so many moths circling a candle.

As each came up, enquiring if I was 'all right', and pressing yet another glass of wine into my hand, I wasn't really seeing them, for all I smiled and nodded and answered their questions. In truth, I was seeing Barry, grinning at me from the kitchen as he chopped an onion; his knife moving with speed and efficiency as it reduced the vegetable to a thousand tiny cubes.

Then he seemed to change – his hair lost its grey and became brown again, thickening until it flopped over one eye. His beard disappeared, and he lost the weight of older age; slimming down until he was once more the lithe, fit young man

I had first met while he was studying theatre design at the Regent Street Poly.

As I sat there, nursing my umpteenth wine, the years seemed to roll away for me as well. I was no longer in the Bistro, coming to grips with losing Barry; now it was a warm June evening in 1958, and I was about to meet him for the first time.

Annie and I were standing outside the magnificent Poly building in Regent Street; its elegant columns rising up from the first floor, with triangular pediments above the windows. We were both excited and nervous at the same time; excited to be going to a 'hop' where there would be boys – lots of them – and nervous for exactly the same reason.

Annie was in a poodle skirt she was most proud of, while I was in a Mary Quant designed dress my mother had created for me. I'd seen the original in Bazaar, Mary Quant's shop in the King's Road, and Mother had agreed to 'knock off' the design. A couple of girls glanced at me as they tripped past, and I fancy I caught a look of appreciation. It thrilled me to think that they might see me as a leader in fashion. Maybe they thought I was a model...

I turned my attention back to the building. "You're absolutely sure there's a hop on tonight?" I asked, probably not for the first time.

"Yes," Annie replied. "I told you, my cousin Adam is studying here, and he said we could come."

"Right," I said. "Let's do this."

Inside, we were shown into the Great Hall, to be greeted by a song I had not heard before (but was to hear a lot more); 'Volare' by Dean Martin. Annie and I stopped just inside the door, taking in the room. The lights were dim, but I could just make out a man in a colourful shirt on the stage, with two record turntables on the desk in front of him. 'Volare' came to an end, and he put on a new song; I think it might have been Frankie Vaughan singing 'Kisses Sweeter Than Wine'.

There were lots of couples dancing, and Annie and I were entranced as we watched the boys spinning the girls round and throwing them about; skirts flying out before the boys deftly caught the girls in their arms.

"My mother wouldn't approve," Annie yelled in my ear. "She says boys shouldn't touch a girl unless they're married."

"Mine's the same," I yelled back. Which is why I hadn't told Mother about Joe Brooks, a boy I'd been 'seeing' recently, who I had met at St Martin's. He had persuaded me to be part of a group photoshoot on the steps of the National Gallery for *Women's Own* magazine – giving me my first taste of modelling.

Joe would often take me to the new coffee bars that were springing up in Soho, and we would sit nursing a coffee each; making them last until the dregs were ice cold. We chatted and cuddled – nothing more – but I knew Mother would have been horrified if she had found out. And it wouldn't have just been her who would have been shocked: my father too, but for a different reason. Joe had a motorbike and would often take me for rides. It was a 1949 Vincent Black Lightning, and he was extremely proud of it. I would clutch him tightly, and neither of us would wear a helmet – this was long before it became the law. As I say, my father would not have approved.

Certainly not one particular day, when Joe put my life, and his, in danger.

We had been riding around London. As we came up the Prince of Wales Drive and the chimneys of Battersea Power Station appeared ahead, I tapped him on the shoulder.

"You can let me off here," I said. "I'll walk the last couple of streets home." It was how I usually left him after a bike ride.

Joe stopped but didn't answer immediately; he was looking to our left at the long straight road leading to Chelsea Bridge in the distance. Unusually, there were no other cars to be seen.

He leaned back and said over his shoulder, "This will do a ton, you know."

"What's a ton?" I asked.

"Hundred miles an hour." He gave me a lopsided grin. "I'll show you if you want. You can just as easily walk from the other side of the bridge."

I had no idea what a ton felt like, but it sounded fun, so I said, "OK then."

"Hang on tight." Joe revved the engine, and I clasped my hands around his waist as tightly as I could. Then he let out the clutch, and I yelled as we were away with such a burst of speed I felt as if I had left my stomach behind.

The houses flicked past in a blur as we accelerated, with the engine screaming like a banshee, and I could not believe how quickly the bridge came up to meet us. Then we were on it, the rails flashing past, and in what seemed like a single heartbeat, we were nearly at the junction at the far end, heading towards the café used by the taxi drivers. Joe grabbed at the brakes, and the bike skittered and juddered as it slowed rapidly. Now I was slammed hard into his back, my face pressed so tightly against the leather of his jacket that I thought it would be stuck forever.

We came to a final stop, and Joe put his foot on the pavement. "There," he said, his voice triumphant. "We hit a hundred and one before I had to brake. Not bad, eh?"

I was beyond speech, trying only to unpeel myself from his jacket. "Hmm," was all I could manage, as I climbed stiffly off the bike and got to the pavement, where I leaned against a lamp post until my legs stopped wobbling.

"Night, Joe," was all I could think to say. Not, *That was so dumb. We could have been killed...*

"Night, Annabelle," he replied, then revved the engine again and was gone.

Not surprisingly, I hadn't much wanted to see Joe after that, and by the time Annie and I got to the hop, he had become merely a memory.

We made our way past the dancers to where a table was laid out with glasses and jugs of what I took to be lemonade (it was). "Where's your cousin?" I asked Annie, as I poured us a couple of glasses.

Annie looked around a moment, then pointed at a lad with sandy hair talking to a taller young man with dark hair falling across one eye. "There he is!" She waved to him. "Adam!"

The record finished. Adam and the other boy came over.

While there were greetings and cousinly hugs between Annie and Adam, I sized up the other one. He was a bit taller than me (especially with his Cuban heels), and I guessed two to three years older. He held my gaze with a small smile and seemed to be appraising me as well.

Adam broke away from Annie and looked from me to the boy and back again with a grin. "This is Barry," he said. "Barry Gregory. He's studying theatre design."

Annie jumped in with, 'My friend, Annabelle Sylvester."

Barry held out his hand, and I shook it. "Hello, Annabelle Sylvester," he said.

Maybe it was the hot touch of his hand. Or maybe the twinkle in his eye. Or even the way the light and shade played across his face, creating beautiful shapes that demanded to be drawn. But as we made contact, a sudden warm feeling flushed over me. It was as if I had known Barry all my life, and yet I needed to know everything about him.

"Hello, Barry Gregory," I replied, knowing then, with absolute certainty, that I had just met the man I was going to marry.

Photograph by Alex Stirling

This was taken in Alex's studio on the King's Road. It was where my modelling career really started; where I first got the bug!

Chapter Six

Becoming A Model (Part 1)

My mother made me leave St Martin's to get a job, which makes me wonder: did missing out on a degree help or hinder my art career? Of course I'll never know; you only go through life once, and the decisions you make – or are made for you – take you on a single path. How can you ever know where a different path might have led?

At the time I do know I was desperately upset to be leaving the school; I was told that my drawings were 'exceptional' – and I had built up real confidence in my own abilities as an artist. I can trace the skills that enabled me to fill the walls of the Bistro with life drawings back to those heady days on the Charing Cross Road, and the joy I felt being able to create art from the human body.

Perhaps if I look at fellow students, I can see what might have been? My classmate Robert Lenkiewicz, for example, went on to the Royal Academy, and although the art establishment never really accepted him, he was popular with the public. His paintings of the down-and-outs he sheltered in his studio became quite collectable, and he produced them at a prolific rate. I remember him as rather a solitary young man; something of a loner, but then, maybe that's the part of the artistic temperament I never had. He died relatively young (at 60), twenty years after he faked his own death as a publicity stunt.

Many of the other students were rich kids, there for a 'jolly' – treating St Martin's as 'a bit of fun' before they met some rich banker and settled down as a good wife and mother. I used to try and avoid them in classes; they were quite disruptive with their braying hyena voices, and for those of us who were there to learn, their behaviour could prevent us from getting on.

But my mother had made it very clear that I did not have the luxury of continuing at St Martin's, and I had to get myself a job. During a brief – and not particularly enjoyable – stint selling knickers, bras and corsets in a shop in the Lansdowne Road, I was offered an interview for a job as an assistant to Alex Stirling, the photographer.

The introduction had come through Barry, whose mother knew someone who knew Alex. She'd found out he was looking for an assistant, and Barry, who knew how unhappy I was in the underwear shop, suggested I go for it.

I followed the address to a building on the King's Road, and when I got there, I was a bit confused. I actually knew it well; it was the Pheasantry – a night club where some of the smartest of the Chelsea set went; a club I had desperately longed to go myself but never had the chance. How could it also be a photography studio?

Come on Annabelle, I said to myself. *You're not going to have to sell a corset to another old biddy if you get this job.* So I took a breath, clutched my portfolio, and went inside.

I was told that Alex Stirling had a studio on the top floor, and was directed up endless flights of stairs, eventually arriving at a door with his name on. Gingerly I pushed it open and poked my head round. Before me was a massive space with white walls and a stripped wooden floor, mainly lit by sunlight coming through several large glass skylights. Everywhere I looked there was jumble; large flat boards leaning against the walls, several fans on stands, lots of lights – some also on stands – while others were perched on wooden crates.

At the far end was a white curtain suspended from the ceiling, which reached all the way to the floor, then spread out towards me. Several lights were set up to point at it. On the floor part of the curtain was a high-backed chair, turned sideways on. Leaning on the chair with one knee on the seat and a hand on the back, was a very curvy blonde, wearing only a black corset and tights. I later found out her name was Sabrina; the model Alex liked to photograph most often. His muse.

Alex himself was a short, stoutish man with his shirt sleeves rolled up, crouching in front of her, snapping away with his camera, as she moved, smiled, pouted and laughed.

"Lovely, my dear," he said, standing back and lowering the camera. "We take the break there." He had a strong accent, which I later found out was Russian.

The blonde must have noticed me over his shoulder, causing the man to turn and see me by the door.

"Annabelle Sylvester," I announced. "Here for the assistant job."

"Oh, ah, yes," he said, coming over to where I stood. "This is your portfolio?"

I nodded, and he held out his hand. He was probably in his early forties, with shaggy black hair and sharp features. I gave it over, and he leafed through. "You can draw," he observed, as he stopped at a couple of life studies. "Where you say you train?"

"St Martin's," I said, neglecting to add that I had only done a Foundation course.

He pursed his lips and nodded.

"OK. Hold out your hand. Keep it still."

Unsure of why he was asking this, I held my right hand out towards him, palm down. He watched it for what must have been a minute, then said, "Good. Very steady. No tremor. You'll do. Start Monday, eight thirty."

I was so excited that I completely forgot to ask why he wanted to see the steadiness of my hand, and it was only the following Monday that I found out.

Alex Stirling hired me mainly as a retouching artist, and also as a photographer's assistant. This meant carrying lights around, making sure they were set up to his exacting satisfaction, and taking notes about each shot so he could identify them when the film came back from processing. It also meant I got to watch Alex work, taking hundreds of shots of the many different models who came in to show off the latest fashions for the glossy magazines, or publicity shots for films or plays.

He would move around the studio with the grace of a ballet dancer, his camera always held up to his face, barking out instructions to the models in his guttural accent. The girls would do whatever he wanted, keeping moving themselves, always maintaining eye contact with the lens. It made me realise that my own preening before my bedroom mirror was just idealised wishful thinking; the model was there to deliver the photographer's vision, not her own. I remember making a mental note as I watched; *when I'm a model, I'll know exactly what I need to do...*

Meanwhile, my other responsibility was the retouching. This was a job that required the stillest of hands, where even the slightest tremor could ruin the work. I don't know whether it was my ability to keep my hand steady for a minute that impressed him, or my skills as an artist. Or perhaps it was both – because they were equally necessary.

Another skill with Alex, was keeping out of the way of his legendary fiery temper. At this, I was usually quite successful – unlike his models, who would often get a severe dressing-down if they didn't do exactly what he wanted.

I took note of what it was that provoked his anger and would often wonder what I would do if I was in their situation. Certainly not wisecrack him, as that was usually what set him off. Or give him a pose that was not exactly what he demanded.

I kept my head down and learned as much as I could from life in the studio, while always doing my best for him – a positive way to keep on his good side. Looking back, I would say he was lucky to have me – not that he recognised it at the time. I think to him, I was in the background, the quiet polite one who just 'got on with it' and always thanked him for my weekly pay packet. This was a very welcome part of my life. It was the first time I was properly paid, rather than 'something from the till' after selling knickers for the week. Once I had given over a proportion to help my mother with the rent, I would treat myself to new clothes. I do recall that at one point the latest fashion was Levi's jeans, so I went from shop to shop trying to find a pair. Sadly, the women's jeans were all sold out, so in the end I settled for a man's pair, which were way too big round the waist and had to be held up by a tight belt, like a set of ruched curtains.

Alex commented on these one day, just as he was heading down to the Pheasantry for lunch with the Italian painter, Annigoni.

"In name of Heaven, Annabelle," he barked. "What is wrong with trousers?"

"They're men's, Alex," I replied, using the simple, direct answer that usually avoided his anger. "And they didn't have my size."

"What I pay you for?" he demanded. "Go buy women's clothes!"

"Will do, Alex."

"And get on with retouch. Have you finished yet?"

"Nearly, Alex. It's quite a complex job. But I'll have it done by the end of the day." Which I did.

I'm told that these days you can retouch any image as quick as you like with a computer (dreadful things – hate them), but with Alex, retouching was very much a manual process that took time, and patience. First, you scraped away part of the photographic image with the edge of a razor blade. This required the tiniest of movements, and the highest concentration. Then you painted in the new part using either inks or pencils (all in black and white), building up the image, and using your abilities as an artist to make it look right.

As Alex's retoucher, I was often asked to make people look younger; to take out frown lines and smooth wrinkles. I used to enjoy watching the actual shoot, trying to work out what I was going to have to change later on. On one occasion a dapper middle-aged man in a dark double-breasted suit came in. He had a pleasant smile, with eyes that twinkled behind his heavy-rimmed glasses. As he sat for Alex, I checked out the wrinkles across his forehead, as well as the crow's feet around his eyes. For a man in his mid-fifties, I felt these should go. I was confident I could remove them and take a fair few years off him – which is what I later did. His name, I found out, was David Brown, the man behind a company making tractors, then Aston Martin cars. I feel honoured to have helped him look his best for the world.

Did this retouching work help advance my artistic career? Did it lessen the pain of having to leave St Martin's? I would say it did; not only because it introduced me to a new type of highly technical artistic expression, but also because it brought me into the world of photography. And this ultimately took me to a whole new life as a model for both fashion and television – working with Cy Endfield, Terence Donovan and Dick Lester.

Although I did get to do some modelling for Alex myself one quiet afternoon. There was no shoot on, and I needed a break from the intensity of the retouching job I was doing. I was sitting at my desk with a glass of water, leafing idly through a fashion magazine, when Alex came over.

"You take break from work, Annabelle?" he asked, sitting at the spare chair beside me. He seemed to be in a pleasant mood, so I nodded and indicated the magazine. He glanced at the page, which had a head and shoulders shot of Pattie Boyd by Donovan. She was all big hair and big mascaraed eyes, giving a sultry stare right down the lens of the camera.

"She is very good, I think," Alex said. His gaze turned to me. "Perhaps you also look good like this? Perhaps I take some shots of you?"

"Oh," I said, "Yes, Alex. That would be great."

"Come then," he said, and led me over to the cove, where the black stool was still there from the previous shoot. We set up the lights, then he had me sit on the stool. He stood back and eyed me critically.

"What is this shirt you wear?" he asked.

"It's a man's dress shirt..." I began, then stopped as his expression turned to a scowl.

"I already tell you this, Annabelle," he growled. "I pay you to look like woman, not man." Then he shook his head and gave me a thin smile. "We carry on regardless." He looked around the studio. "But we use the props, yes? In the background." He pointed at a bunch of balloons floating on the end of a string. "Bring those." Then he noticed a rocking horse hiding behind a couple of lights. "And that. Help bring it over."

Once these were positioned to his satisfaction behind me, Alex was ready. He put the camera to his face, and suddenly it was me on the receiving end of his instructions. "Turn to left, Annabelle! Now to right! Shoulders back, relax, relax! There's good, Lovely! And again! Smile! Now sexy pout! That's good, Annabelle, that's good!"

Then it was over.

"I show you pictures when developed," he said. "Now get back to work."

The 2is Coffee Bar

I found these pictures on the internet and was immediately taken back to the 2is at 59 Old Compton Street, Soho.

Photos courtesy of nostalgiacentral.com.

Chapter Seven

Becoming Part Of The Soho Coffee Culture

Barry was in many ways the opposite of me. Maybe, as they say, opposites attract.

While we did have a fair bit in common, such as an appreciation of the burgeoning rock scene and the new Soho coffee-bar culture, Barry was from a completely different background. His family were as well-off as mine were not. He had been educated at Rugby School, although he took it as a source of pride that he'd been kicked out. After that, he'd gone to Paris and enrolled in the Sorbonne, where, from what I could gather, he seemed to spend most of his time in Parisian cafes with a succession of French girls.

Barry's father was a senior executive in the UK division of an American chemical company, who was divorced from Barry's mother. His father's new partner was Cynthia Tingey, a noted costumier who worked for Bermans and designed for entertainers like Cilla Black and Danny La Rue, as well as for films like Cliff Richard's *Summer Holiday*.

My time with Alex Stirling seemed to have run its natural course, especially when I decided that the strain of walking on eggshells around his temper was becoming way too stressful. So Cynthia got me a job at Bermans as a runner. This meant going all over Soho; into the fabric stores, shoe dye workshops and haberdashers, picking up bits of fabric, braids and accessories that had been made or adapted locally so the team at Bermans could create their amazing theatrical costumes.

Of course, being Soho, there were also some shady goings-on; one particular shoe-dye place was in a little attic room above a brothel. You had to pick your way up the stairs, past the queue of men waiting their turn. Most of the men looked quite cagey and a bit embarrassed; but it was the ones who didn't – the confident ones – who would try and pinch my bottom as I went past. Needless to say, I had a set of stock responses I used on a regular basis.

I got to know the Soho area well, and particularly the coffee bars springing up all over West London – which Barry and I would visit often.

Our favourite haunt was the 2is Coffee Bar in Old Compton Street, which was to London in the late fifties/early sixties, what the Cavern Club was to Liverpool. There was a tiny basement with a small stage, and room for about twenty people to watch the acts – although I was sure there were often a lot more crammed in. The heat – and the smell – could be pretty ghastly. But the acts were fantastic, so that made it all worth it. By the time Barry and I started going, some of the original acts had moved up to the big time, while the talent scouts were always finding new ones to take their place. Tommy Steele and the Cavemen had been discovered there, but were now too big for it, while Cliff Richard was still appearing occasionally with his Shadows. I remember at the time thinking that he was just another pretty young lad, like Tommy Steele and Joe Brown.

We would stand at the counter, drinking coffee from transparent cups, and watching to see who was there. I do remember one little fellow in a halter-top vest, who had a lot more thick black hair on his shoulders and arms than on his head. I couldn't help thinking of a mountain bear I once had seen in a copy of the *National Geographic* magazine. Barry seemed to know him and introduced me one evening.

"Annabelle, this is Lionel. Lionel Bart. He's a songwriter."

"Oh yes," I said, eyeing him over the rim of my coffee cup. "And what songs have you written?" I expected him to name something obscure, but he shrugged, as if such questions were almost demeaning.

"'Rock with the Caveman'," he said.

I gave a small gasp – that was Tommy Steele's first major hit; one I had rushed out and bought as soon as it was released. "Wow," I said. "That's pretty impressive."

Lionel shrugged again. "Cliff and the Shads did quite well with my 'Living Doll'."

I gasped again and glanced at Barry. I think he was quite enjoying how impressed I was by his acquaintance. "Anything else?" I asked.

"I'm working on something new; a musical show. I've nearly finished all the songs, and I'm quite pleased with it." Lionel paused. "I've got a good feeling about this one. I think it's going to be a hit."

"What's the show about?" Barry asked.

"It's an adaptation of *Oliver Twist* by Dickens."

"Sounds great," I said. I'd no idea what a musical show was, but it seemed exciting. And *Oliver Twist* was a good subject. I'd read the book and been struck by the tale of the orphaned boy, as it reminded me of when my family first arrived in London and I was sent to live away with my Nan.

Lionel nodded to us then left, pushing through the crowd. Barry turned to me. "I'll take you to see it, when it comes out, if you like." Which he did – and I loved every second of *Oliver!* I still hum 'Consider Yourself' while I'm painting, even now.

After the 2is, we'd often go on to have a drink and a meal at Tiddy Dols Eating House. This was a bar and restaurant in Mayfair's Shepherd Market which looked like it had stepped straight out of the Dickensian London that Lionel Bart was recreating. The front window was made up of many small square panes of glass, and there was a bell on the front door that tinkled wonderfully when you went in. It was always warm and cosy inside, and we would have a few drinks there, and maybe one of their famous Welsh Rarebits.

Our other haunts included Le Macabre on Wardour Street, which had tables in the shape of coffins. There was jive dancing, and occasionally some beatniks would get up and declaim their weird poetry. Barry would often get into a heated political debate with some worthy communist; while he was generally quite relaxed in his political views, he loved to play up his public-school education and take an opposing position to a left-winger. I remember on one occasion, we had to get out fairly quickly, before a group of communists set on us.

Another place we'd go to was the Partisan Coffee House in Carlisle Street – which was a hotbed of left-wing extremism. Barry knew better than to play up his Rugby schooling there; it was founded as a radical intellectual hangout, so there wouldn't have been any debate – we'd have been thrown out immediately. But there were some interesting people; Ken Tynan the theatre critic could be seen discussing the latest 'kitchen sink' drama with Michael Redgrave, while screenwriter Wolf Mankowitz, who was noted for his interest in antiques and pottery, would engage people on these subjects. He once sat Barry down and explained the antiques trade to him. At the time Barry seemed not to be particularly keen – but it must have sparked an interest, as we ended up in the antiques business ourselves many years later.

On another occasion, Wolf Mankowitz introduced us to his sister, Barbara, a solid, no-nonsense woman in the china business in Piccadilly. She had a young colleague with her, a woman who had come down from Grimsby a couple of years earlier. Recently married, she announced she was now expecting her first baby, and we all congratulated her.

Barry and I discussed this later. "It made me wonder," I told him. "I think I'd like to have kids."

He smiled and stroked my cheek. "Of course, Annabelle."

I paused, looking deeply into his eyes. Was this going to be the moment he would propose? I held my breath and waited in anticipation, mentally starting to try on wedding gowns and choose bridesmaids. But Barry just smiled again, and murmured, "I think you'd make a great mum."

The subject was left there, and I had to 'step away' from the wedding gown rail.

That was until the Gregory family invited me to join them on a summer holiday in Saint-Tropez.

My father and his Fiat Taxis

I found this picture on a website celebrating the Fiat Multipla – which my father used for his fleet of taxis. It was strange seeing this picture of him online – looking very dapper in his double-breasted suit. His taxi business was going on while I was starting to live my own life – particularly holidaying in St-Tropez
with Barry and his family.

Photo courtesy of the Fiat 600 Multipla Registry.

Chapter Eight

Becoming a Jet-Setter

We flew out from London Airport to Nice on a magnificent aeroplane. I'd never flown before (we'd gone to Alderney by boat), but as a small child I had often seen the planes coming in to land at Croydon Airport while I was in the garden at Whyteleafe. I wondered what it would be like to fly in one.

Well, now I was going to find out. As we walked out of the terminal and over to the plane in its stylish black and white Air France livery, Barry leaned down and said, "It's a Caravelle. A new model; the latest in flying. And we're going First Class." I looked up and nodded, my throat tight with a mix of excitement and fear.

"Have you flown before?" I asked in a small voice.

"Oh yes," he replied. "Lots of times when I was at the Sorbonne." He considered me a moment, then took my hand. "You'll love it, Annabelle. It's a magical experience." I gripped him tightly as we all walked across to the plane. There was a stewardess seeing the passengers up the steps, and I paused slightly to admire her uniform. She was in a figure-hugging dark navy suit, single breasted, with a narrow skirt. Underneath was a white poplin blouse. On her head she wore a black felt beret with a smart gold crest, and she was holding a black shoulder bag in her white gloved hand. I could not believe a uniform could be so stylish.

Perhaps I was going to enjoy this.

She gave me a big smile and said. "Bonjour Mam'selle."

I smiled back and looked up the stairs, having sudden doubts about going aboard. Barry squeezed my hand and led me up them; my legs feeling quite wobbly. At the top we were greeted by another smiling stewardess who checked our boarding passes and directed us to our seats. These were at the front of the plane, just before a grey curtain separating us from the rest of the passengers.

"You're in the window seat," Barry said. "You'll get an amazing view."

I sat down and immediately felt better. Barry sat next to me, then showed me how to do up my belt. His sister, Avril, was on the other side and leaned across. "It's the only way to travel," she said with a grin. "It's so exciting!"

And she was right. As the engines roared and the plane started its take-off, we were pressed back so hard into our seats I could hardly breathe – but that was all part of the thrill. The fields outside the triangle-shaped window raced past, reminding me of Joe Brooks on his bike. Then we were up in the air, and the fields became smaller and smaller, until suddenly they disappeared in a white cloudy mist that flicked past – and then we were out into blazing sunshine, with a thick carpet of clouds below us.

Barry touched my arm. "I told you it's magical," he said.

"It's amazing," I replied, looking down at the clouds. They appeared solid enough to walk on. I settled back in my seat as a stewardess came by with some glasses of Champagne.

Oh yes, I was definitely going to enjoy this...

Two days later I was stretched out on my sun lounger, feeling the hot South of France sun beating down on my closed eyes. This was the life! For a girl from Whyteleafe, Croydon, to be in a luxury hotel near Saint-Tropez, seemed unbelievable. But here I was, guest of Barry's father and Cynthia, staying with the whole family in the Hotel Cavalière and relaxing on its private beach. The family seemed to have accepted me wholeheartedly, and although I was cautious at first, the friendliness of their welcome and inclusion in conversations meant I soon felt as if I fully belonged.

Barry's voice interrupted my thoughts. "Do you fancy a drink, Annabelle?"

I opened my eyes. A dark shape towered over me, silhouetted against the bright light. I squinted at him, sat up, then put on my sun hat and dark glasses. "A Champagne would be lovely," I said.

"Coming right over," he replied, and raised a hand to attract a waiter's attention.

"I seem to be developing a taste for it," I admitted, once he'd ordered.

I looked out to sea. It was so inviting, twinkling beyond the empty beach. I'd been in the clear waters several times already, swimming out from the beach, then coming back and splashing about with Avril, Clive, Cynthia and Barry in the shallows. I had enjoyed the feeling of the soft sand beneath my toes as we threw a beach ball to each other. Somehow Barry always seemed to end up playfully picking me up and throwing me under the waves. I'd come up spluttering and laughing, then try and push him under myself, so we'd end up wrestling in the shallows.

My mother would have been shocked at such brazen intimacy, but none of Barry's family seemed to have any problem with it.

It was as if they already had us engaged – which was such a lovely thought.

Except that Barry still hadn't actually asked.

The Champagne arrived and was poured. We clinked glasses and sipped, then I looked Barry deep in the eyes. "Saint-Tropez is such a romantic place," I said, lowering my voice a tone or two. "I could get used to holidays like this. It would be a great place to bring kids." I lowered my eyes briefly, then looked up at him again. "Our kids..."

He was silent a moment, seeming deep in thought, as he stared back.

Then he seemed to have made up his mind.

"Annabelle Sylvester," he said. "Will you marry me?"

※

Everyone was so excited that we were finally engaged, (I'd said "yes", of course, but had first given Barry a long pause, as if I had to think about it). There was plenty more Champagne, and our health was toasted many times.

That evening we were sitting up at the bar enjoying our drinks, when Barry nudged me and indicated the man sitting on his other side.

"That's Victor Silvester, the band leader," he whispered.

I made a surreptitious glance across. The man beyond him was a tall, well-dressed fellow with dark hair, talking to a pretty blonde. He looked to be in his mid-thirties. "I thought he was older than that," I whispered back, thinking of the picture of the dapper older fellow on the cover of a record I'd got at home. "He looks too young."

"It's Victor Junior," Barry explained. "The son." He turned to Victor Silvester and introduced himself, then indicated me. "And this is my fiancée, Annabelle. She works at Bermans."

"Oh, the costumier?" Silvester asked. I nodded, wordlessly basking in the glow of Barry introducing me as 'his fiancée'.

"And this is my wife, Marlene." The blonde gave me a smile, and came round to my side, as Barry and Victor started talking together.

"You work at Bermans?" she asked, and I nodded. "I don't model their stuff," she said.

"Oh, you're a model?" I asked. She certainly had the figure for it.

"Yes." She smiled again. "It's such fun. You get to wear some great outfits and get paid for showing them off." She stood back and looked me up and down, then observed, "You could be a model, Annabelle. Have you ever thought of it?"

"I have actually," I admitted with a shy smile. "Before Bermans I worked for Alex Stirling in his studio and loved the way the girls came out all dressed up for him to shoot."

"And you thought – 'I could do that'?"

"I did." For a moment the Saint-Tropez bar faded away, and I was once again back in Alex's studio, staring down the lens as Alex photographed me that afternoon.

Then I was watching from the side as girls like his famous muse model, Sabrina, came out. She looked so stylish in her breathtaking outfits, sashaying across the floor like she was on the runway in Paris, before twisting, turning and smiling as she posed for the camera... Then even that image faded as well, and I was staring at the reflection of my teenage self in my bedroom mirror, pouting and turning as I imagined a photographer encouraging me with instructions on the poses he wanted...

"You should give it a go," Marlene said, bringing me back to the present with a start. "I think you'd be a natural." She gave me another smile and went over to her husband. Barry and I returned to our drinks, as she and Victor left the bar.

"She thought I should try modelling," I told Barry.

He gave a small shrug. "If you want. Why not?"

I twirled my glass, watching how the bubbles rose up like strings of tiny pearls. I took a sip, then put the glass down firmly on the bar. "Then that's what I'm going to do," I said. "I'm going to be a model."

On the last day of the two weeks, we had some further – and very welcome – news.

We were having a drink on the terrace when Barry's father and Cynthia came up.

"Hello, you two," Cynthia said, as she put her bag down by her feet and settled into one of the other chairs at our table. "How have you been enjoying the life of an engaged couple?"

Barry's father eased his bulk into the other spare chair. "Now then, Cyn," he said. "Let's not put any pressure on the youngsters." Then he raised an eyebrow at us. "Although I have noticed you both sneaking off together a few times." He gave a rather obvious wink, which made me squirm with embarrassment. Barry, however, was unfazed.

"Just sampling the local eateries, Dad," he said. "Nothing more than that."

"Of course," his father replied, although thankfully he didn't repeat the wink. And Barry was right, we had been trying out different restaurants, which Barry saw as much as research for the new place he had been setting up with his father in Dover Street. They called it the 31 Room, and Barry was very excited to be making his first foray into the world of hospitality.

A waiter came up. Barry's father ordered Champagne and four glasses. I gave an enquiring look at Barry, but he seemed as unaware as I was as to what his father and Cynthia were planning to celebrate. Given how much fizz had been drunk since we'd announced our engagement, I could hardly imagine that this was once again the cause.

Once the waiter had left, Cynthia glanced at Barry's father as if for approval to begin. He nodded, so she said, "We have something to offer you. For the wedding."

"What's that?" Barry asked, while I ran through a few things in my mind. *A honeymoon holiday? A cake? The wedding car?* Although that should really be my own father. *What else could it be?*

"Robert and I want you both to have one of the flats we own in Ebury Street."

There was a stunned silence, interrupted by the waiter arriving and pouring the Champagne. His father raised his glass. "To your first home as a married couple."

I couldn't think of anything to say as we sipped our fizz – apart from running round and giving them both a massive hug. To have a place of our own! And in such a great part of London! That was more than I could possibly have hoped for.

"You mean it?" Barry asked. "Really?"

Cynthia nodded over the rim of her glass. "Of course."

Barry's mind went to the practicalities. "You'll want rent, of course?"

His father shrugged. "Peppercorn only. Property values are on the up, so it's worth us hanging on to it as an investment. No mortgage or anything."

There was another silence. I was aware of Barry looking at me, as if he was expecting me to say something. But I was incapable of speech at that moment; such generosity by my fiancé's family was quite beyond me.

"Well?" Cynthia asked.

"I... um..." I tried, but the words wouldn't come. The opportunity to move out of the flat in Warwick Square, where I had been living with my mother, seemed a dream.

So I went round and hugged them both. It seemed the right thing to do.

My mother and I had been sharing the flat in Warwick Square, together with Ingrid and Charlotte. My philandering father had left us by this time, and they'd got divorced.

I'm not sure which was worse for him, getting the divorce, or having to give up the billiard room he'd been using as a radio taxi control room to run his cab business. I say 'the' billiard room, in fact it was 'a' billiard room, as it was not actually part of our flat. He'd found a way into it via a secret connecting door, and no-one had ever stopped him using it. Being the chancer he was, he'd set up all his equipment and was happily using it to manage all the cabs. I would often put my ear to the door to hear his booming voice with conversations like: "Come in Sixty-four. Sixty-four. Pick-up 14 Manchuria Road, Clapham. 3 p.m. Over." Then later, a crackly voice saying, "This is Sixty-four. Manchuria Road. POB. I repeat, POB, over." That was 'passenger on board', apparently.

Before my mother had thrown him out, his business had been fighting what became known as the 'taxi wars' – which even inspired a film; *Carry On Cabby*. A man called Michael Gotla had launched his Welbeck Motors mini-cab company, with a fleet of two hundred bright red Renault Dauphines. These made my father's modest fleet of twenty-five black and white Fiat Multiplas seem almost quaint by comparison. It was not so much that my father couldn't compete with Welbeck (although he couldn't, especially as Gotla undercut him at a shilling a mile), it was that Welbeck caused the established London black cabs to rise up in arms. My father, who had previously been small enough to fly under the black cabs' radar, got caught in the crossfire.

Eventually it went to court. On 31 May 1962, a court ruling determined that some of my father's drivers had been 'plying for hire', in violation of the law that protected the black cabs. Father had to stop his taxi operation, until eventually the laws changed and he could get started again.

To this day I cannot watch the 1963 film *Carry On Cabby* (which was actually filmed in Windsor, doubling for London), without being taken back to that billiard room.

But now my father had gone, and my mother was becoming ever more demanding, which I was finding harder and harder to manage. So the thought that I could move out, and Barry and I could have a place to ourselves, was beyond my wildest dreams.

A dream that was now coming true, in the warmth of the Saint-Tropez sun.

"Thank you, thank you" I said to Barry's father, then hugged Cynthia again.

It was all arranged. A date was set for the wedding in 1961, and after that, we were going to move into the Ebury Street flat.

And somehow, I was going to become a model.

We set off the next day. I took a last look as we were driven through Saint-Tropez towards Nice Airport. Little did I know I would be back there in only a few days.

As a professional model.

'Party in the Bar'

Oil on canvas. 61cm x 70cm.

Every night was a party in the Bistro, so seeing this painting took me back to the parties that Barry and I went to in London in the late 50s and early 60s.

Chapter Nine

Becoming A Model (Part 2)

The day after we got back, we were invited to a party – I don't particularly remember where – given by a man called Dick Norton. He was a continuity announcer on the TV, and when he and his wife, Jilly, had been introduced to us at one of Cynthia's parties, they seemed to have taken to us.

We got ready at Barry's flat. "There'll be lots of people from film and television," he said as he pulled on one of his Chelsea boots. "Maybe someone who could help you get into modelling."

I looked across at him, curling tongs in hand. "That would be useful." I had taken to doing what was then called 'The Flip', a flicked-up curl at the end of my bob. It had become quite the craze after pictures of Jackie Kennedy had appeared in the papers, and I wanted to be at the front of fashion. I put the tongs down and gave him a smile. "How do I look?"

He finished pulling on the other boot, and stood in front of me, his hands on his hips and his trademark grin making the corners of his mouth turn up. "Pretty as a picture, Annabelle," he said. "But maybe a little more lipstick?"

"I'm not actually wearing any," I replied.

"Oh." He raised an eyebrow. But perhaps he had a point. While I never wore make-up if I could help it, this might be one of those occasions when it would be sensible.

"OK," I said, and put some on.

When we arrived at the party, we were pounced on by Jilly Norton. "Hello darlings!" she cried, thrusting some wine into our hands. "Anyone who's anyone is here. They're just dying to meet you!"

She dragged Barry by the hand across the room, and I followed. Helen Shapiro was singing 'Walkin' Back to Happiness' from the record player as we moved through the throng of people drinking, laughing and shouting over the noise. Some were helping themselves to food from a buffet, while others were dancing, swaying close to each other as Helen sang. Almost everyone was smoking, and a fug of cigarette smoke hung over all the heads.

"Here," Jilly said, stopping in front of two men. One was middle-aged with short dark hair swept back off a high forehead, while the other was balding with thick-rimmed glasses. "Redvers Kyle," Jilly announced, indicating the balding man. He turned and gave us a slightly vague smile. "Redvers works with Dick at Associated-Rediffusion. He presents *Looking and Seeing*; the programme for kids."

Redvers nodded, as Jilly said, "This is Barry Gregory; he has just opened a restaurant in Dover Street called the 31 Room." She waved a hand at me, "And his gorgeous fiancé, Annabelle."

The restaurant had been going well so far, but it meant Barry was out every day from mid-morning through to the early hours. This left me free after work at Bermans to attend life drawing classes and do my own painting at home in Warwick Square; something my mother thought was a waste of time and frequently told me so. This had put quite a strain on our relationship.

Moving with Barry to the flat in Ebury Street couldn't come soon enough.

As Jilly swept away, her hostess job complete, Redvers raised an eyebrow. "You look very young to run a restaurant," he observed in a thick South African accent, taking a long drag on his cigarette and blowing the smoke upwards.

Barry seemed to ignore the implied criticism. "It's early days, but I am confident it's going to be a success," he said. "We've secured a top chef, and we've started getting some great reviews." He paused, glancing up at the pall of smoke. "We even have an outside patio. It's one of the few places in the heart of London where you can drink or dine in the open air. You must come and try it."

As Barry and Redvers continued talking, I became aware that the other man was staring at me. It was a look of interest rather than anything more overt, but it did make me feel slightly uncomfortable. I thought he was probably mid-forties. "Cy Endfield," he announced, with an American twang. It was said with a slight air of self-satisfaction, as if he was sure I had already heard of him. As it happened, I had; his name had come up a few times while I was working for Alex Stirling. He was apparently a film and theatre director who had come over after the McCarthy hearings had put him on the Hollywood blacklist and stopped him being able to work in the USA.

"Annabelle Sylvester," I said.

He regarded me a moment longer, then said, "You look very brown. A healthy glow."

I smiled. "Barry and I have just got back from a holiday in Saint-Tropez."

He nodded. "And what do you do, Annabelle Sylvester, when you're not holidaying in the South of France?" After I told him about Bermans, he observed, "You're wasted running around Soho doing errands. A girl like you should be in front of a camera."

For a moment my breath caught in my throat, while out of the corner of my eye I saw Barry pause in his conversation and glance across at Cy Endfield.

"Yes, I'd like that," I said, nodding. Was this my chance?

He appeared to come to a decision. "I've been given a shoot for Player's cigarettes, and we're looking for a pretty young girl. It's for a TV ad, with the line 'Young People Smoke Player's'. Would you be interested in auditioning?"

Unable to speak, I just nodded.

"OK, come along tomorrow morning. It's at the agency; Doyle, Dane, Bernbach." He gave an address in West London. "Be there at ten."

꧁꧂

At nine forty-five the next morning, I stood outside the grand offices of the Doyle, Dane, Bernbach agency, also known as DDB. I had hardly slept the night before; tossing and turning with my head full of excitement that the opportunity I wanted seemed to have come along so soon.

But now I was actually at the audition, my excitement evaporated like a morning mist. Now it turned to fear. What if I messed up? What if I was fooling myself that I could ever be a model? What if I was laughed out of the audition? My dream would be over.

Much easier to walk back to Bermans and get on with my job.

Come on Annabelle. This is exactly what you wanted. You can do this.

I walked up the steps and through the door. When I got inside, I gasped in wonderment. The foyer was truly magnificent; an imposing space full of marble, massive plants and posters advertising things like Volkswagen motors, Player's and Avis car hire.

A girl behind the massive reception desk looked up enquiringly and said, "Can I help you?"

"I have a meeting with Cy Endfield."

"Which brand is that on?" she asked.

"Player's."

"Oh, right. Third floor. Take the lift."

When I arrived, another girl was waiting. She showed me into a small room, where Cy and a couple of men in sharp suits were sitting behind a desk. A chap in a black polo shirt was crouched beside a cine camera on a tripod, while a couple of studio lights were positioned in the corners. They were trained on a spot in front of the desk, that had a fine Persian carpet. Everyone was smoking, and there were several packs of Player's, lighters and some ashtrays on the desk.

"Hello, Annabelle," Cy said in a reassuring and friendly voice. After he had introduced me to the sharp suits, who were apparently ad men from the agency, he gave me a piece of paper with some lines typed on it, then tapped out a cigarette from a pack and handed it over. As I put it in my mouth, the girl who had shown me in rushed up, flipped open a Zippo lighter, and lit it for me.

There was a whirring noise as the camera was started, and Cy said, "Stand a bit further back please Annabelle, and read those lines to the camera."

I glanced down at the paper. I took a drag of the cigarette, blew slowly out, looked straight down the lens and said: "As a young person, I always reach for the smooth, satisfying taste of Player's. It's mild, rich, and just what I need." I looked down a moment, then back at the camera and added, "Young people smoke Player's."

There was a small laugh from one of the sharp suits. "That's the voice-over line, not hers."

Cy Endfield shook his head. "Don't blame her, it's written on the paper." He leaned across and took a cigarette for himself, lit it, then blew out the smoke. "Good camera appeal, though. Healthy brown tan."

As they all studied me, I wanted to say, *I can hear you, you know. And I'm not a horse being assessed for sale!*

Cy took another drag, and said, "Turn to the left, Annabelle. Now look back at the camera over your shoulder."

I turned with a smile and made a little laugh, then Cy's smoking gave me an idea. I took another drag on my own cigarette and blew smoke at the camera. There were appreciative noises from behind the desk. "Now the same," Cy said, "but from the right."

After a few more instructions, which I seemed to perform to their satisfaction, they went into a huddle, while I stood, not quite sure what to do. The cigarette burned down, and I needed to flick the ash. I glanced down at the fine carpet, and hesitated. Cy and the suits were deep in conversation, so I didn't want to lean over the table and use one of the ashtrays, in case they thought I was trying to overhear them. The ash grew longer. Should I tap it into my hand? Thankfully just as it was about to fall, the girl came over with an ashtray.

"How many others have they seen?" I whispered, as I stubbed the cigarette out. I hoped she'd say, "only a couple."

She shrugged. "Ten. Twelve, perhaps."

"Oh! That's a lot..." I could feel my hopes for a modelling career going up in smoke. What chance would I have against all those girls, who were bound to have plenty of TV experience?

She glanced across at the desk. Cy had just thumped his fist down with a scowl at the suits and sat back with his arms folded. Then the suits leaned across and seemed to be capitulating. Cy nodded, turning to me with a smile. "Annabelle, you said you've just got back from Saint-Tropez?"

"Yes."

"You'd best not have unpacked." His smile broadened. "Because you're going straight back there, to shoot a TV ad."

Photograph of me in the dress bought by Cy Endfield, St-Tropez, 1960

Photo by Desmond Russell.

Buying this dress and doing the Player's shoot in France opened my eyes to the world of professional modelling. Such a beautiful world!

Chapter Ten

Becoming A Model (Part 3)

Two days later I was flicking through the dresses on a rail in a smart Saint-Tropez boutique looking for something to wear on the shoot. Cy and I had flown out that morning, coming straight to the city in a car he'd hired at the airport.

A short pink number with a white lace collar caught my eye, so I picked it out and held it up for Cy. He was sitting in the 'bored man' chair in the corner behind me, idly smoking. He made an expression of mock surprise, then shook his head. With an exaggerated sigh, I went back to my search. This was the third one he'd pooh-poohed. Then I stopped, my hand on a stylish sleeveless dress in grey and white. With a small frisson of excitement I eased it off the rail. It had a nipped-in waist, a full striped skirt, a fitted bodice and a square neck with fine straps. I took it to the mirror and held it to my front. It had the 'French girl' feel of Brigitte Bardot – and I loved it.

"Cy," I called over my shoulder. "Now this one is perfect. You have to admit." He looked up as I turned to show it off, then he raised an eyebrow and nodded with an approving smile. I made a small pirouette and asked to try it on.

As the sales woman zipped it up in the changing room, I smoothed it down, then took a step away from the mirror so I could see it in all its glory. The elegant-looking girl who smiled back from the mirror was quite the sophisticate; the dress giving her a fashionable silhouette and setting off her blonde hair and warm tan.

She was a model.

I gave myself a quiet smile of triumph. Was it only a week ago that Marlene Silvester had suggested I try modelling? And now here I was, wearing a stunning dress in a Saint-Tropez boutique, with a film director beyond the curtain ready to pay for it, and an ad shoot due to start in a hillside château.

Life was good. No, strike that. Life was great.

"Magnifique, mam'selle," the sales woman breathed in my ear. "Très, très jolie. The Monsieur, 'ee will love this."

And Monsieur Endfield, 'ee absolutely did. When I stepped out of the booth and showed it off, he stood up, shook his head with a small whistle, and slowly clapped. "Perfect, Annabelle," he said. "Perfect. Sophisticated, aspirational, and absolutely says you're the kind of young person Player's want to appeal to." He paused a moment, then asked the woman, "How much is it?"

She named a price, and I quickly calculated what that was in pounds and shillings. I froze. It was twice what I had made at Bermans in a month! How could Cy possibly afford it?

But he just nodded, took out his wallet, and started counting out the franc notes.

I watched in disbelief as he handed them over.

"You'd better get changed back, Annabelle," he said, seeming not to notice my amazement. "We need to be at the château in an hour as I have to set up the shoot."

With some difficulty, I made my legs carry me over to the changing room.

As we walked along the pavement back to the car in the glorious sunshine, I swung the bag and said, "Thank you so much, Cy. I love it."

"Don't thank me," he said. "Thank Player's and DDB."

I glanced into the bag, where the many layers of tissue wrapping could just be seen. "Well, 'thank you' to Player's and DDB. It's beautiful."

Cy gave me a sideways glance, and with a start, I realised something I hadn't noticed before. He was perfectly safe. Many men would have used that as a lead-in line. *Well, you're beautiful, Annabelle. Let's have dinner together, just the two of us...* In fact, my mother had warned me before I left, saying, "Those film people, my girl; the men are only after one thing. You be extra careful."

But it was clear to me that Cy Endfield was not like that. He was not only a consummate professional, he was also charming and totally trustworthy. And he had let me have what was probably the most expensive dress in the shop without a murmur.

As I said, life was great.

Château Minuty was on a steep hillside, with fields of vines stretching out on both sides, and the beautiful Gulf of Saint-Tropez laid out below like a perfect picture postcard. The deep blue of the sea was surrounded by the Côte d'Azur, with Port Grimaud on the left and Saint-Tropez itself over to the right.

When we arrived by taxi, the cast and crew were busy setting up. Unshaven men in singlets and berets were hauling around lights on stands, positioning them on the gravel in front of the château itself. This was a wide, two-storey building with cream-painted walls and an orange tiled roof; not what I would have thought of as a château at all. I suppose I had expected a fairy-tale castle, like the ones in the Disney cartoons I had seen at the cinema as a girl. But this was still pretty special.

Two men were laying what looked like a small railway track, running from the front steps towards a couple of tall decorative bushes that led into beautifully manicured gardens.

"We won't be shooting for a while," Cy said to me, as he took in the scene, "but I'll need to stay here to oversee the set-up. You and the other cast can go into Ramatuelle for lunch. There's a great restaurant there called Au Soleil. Maxine will take you. It's worth it for the view alone. We won't need you for a few hours."

As if on cue, a woman in her mid-thirties in a flowery sundress and large-brimmed hat came up. "Maxine," Cy said, "this is Annabelle." He turned to me. "Maxine is the Assistant Producer; she works for the film company hired by DDB. She'll take you and the other cast members up to Ramatuelle."

"Come on dear," Maxine said. "I'll drive you up." She led me round the side of the building to where an old Citroen was standing. Two beautifully dressed girls and a boy, all about my age, were leaning against it, chatting and smoking. Maxine led me up to them. "This is Linda, and this is Barbara," she said. "And this is Colin." She paused. "Annabelle, everyone."

Linda and Barbara seemed to barely register my arrival, but Colin said, "Hello Annabelle. I hear you're the new face of Player's?"

At this, Linda looked me up and down with barely concealed distaste. "The new face of Player's?" she repeated. "What shoots have you done, then?"

I forced a smile and said in what I hoped was my warmest voice, "None so far; this is my first." But it seemed to have been a waste of effort. Barbara gave a snort and exclaimed to Linda, "Her first? And she gets the lead?" She shook her head, as if unable to believe what she'd heard.

I was trying to think of a suitable reply, when Maxine said, "Come now girls, let's all play nicely. We'll be together for the week, and we've got an ad to shoot."

As we settled in the car, with Colin in the front beside Maxine and me between the two girls in the back, I couldn't avoid a sinking feeling. Cy might be friendly and trustworthy, but if Linda and Barbara were going to be snooty cows, it could turn the week I was expecting to enjoy into a potentially unpleasant one.

"What shoots have you done?" I asked Linda, in the brightest, most friendly tone I could manage. Unfortunately it had as little effect as before.

"Lots, new girl," she said, looking away out of the window as we drove through the glorious countryside. "Lots and lots. More than you'll ever do."

Barbara cut in before I could reply. "And she didn't have to be so generous of her time with the director." She paused for a beat. "If you know what I mean."

I gasped at the insinuation, as Maxine brought the car to a sudden stop. "Woah, there," she snapped, turning in her seat to stare at Barbara. "Woah," she repeated. "That was totally uncalled for. I won't have insinuations like that flying around, you hear?" Barbara said nothing, so Maxine continued, "You say sorry to Annabelle. Right now. Or I turn this car round and drive you straight back to the airport." Barbara said nothing. "I mean it," Maxine insisted.

Barbara took a breath and muttered, "Sorry Annabelle."

"It's OK," I said, seeing the chance to be magnanimous. "But I can assure you I wouldn't do anything like that."

Maxine nodded, and drove on, while Linda muttered, almost so quietly I didn't hear, "So you say."

After driving up a hill with many consecutive hairpin bends, we arrived in Ramatuelle. As the others went ahead into the restaurant, Colin pulled me to one side, and said, "I wouldn't worry too much about them. They're just a bit pissed off you got the lead and neither of them did."

"All I did was audition," I replied. "I didn't know what role it was for."

He gave a small shrug. "Well, it is what it is. Just be yourself, Annabelle, and I'm sure it will all work out in the end."

And of course, he was right. Over the next few days we shot the scenes for the ad, with me and Colin as the couple surrounded by our two other 'friends'; all relaxing, laughing and smoking Player's cigarettes for the cameras. Gradually the forced laughter on set became more genuine laughter off it, as we shared the experience of take after take; repeated instructions from Cy (who at least did not have Alex Stirling's temper), and plenty of drinks at the end of each day. Eventually the barriers seemed to come down. Colin and I took to having a stroll through the harbour in the evenings, admiring the amazing yachts and having a drink in the bars that lined the pavement. I won't say that Linda or Barbara ever became firm friends, but at least we ended the week on easier terms.

And one thing that Linda said that was definitely wrong – I went on to make many, many more ads than she ever did, including lots of Player's ads with Colin.

The work continued; there was even one evening where I appeared in five different ads in one break. By then my modelling career had really taken off, aided mainly by Jilly Norton. She had effectively become my agent, proving adept at finding me lots of work.

Which meant I was juggling modelling assignments with being the fiancé, then the wife, of Barry Gregory, the noted London restaurateur.

Wedding Party group outside St. Peter's Eaton Square, 11 November 1961

This picture was in a family album. There were lots of smiles and love that day – and a few upsets too.

Chapter Eleven

Becoming Mrs Gregory

My mother was shocked about the way Barry had proposed. "What do you mean, 'he just asked'?" she demanded when I had first told her my momentous news. "Why didn't he go down on one knee and give you the ring? And why didn't he ask your father's permission first?"

"To be fair," I pointed out. "Dad's gone off somewhere with another of his floozies, and we were in the South of France at the time. It wouldn't have been possible."

"Then this Barry of yours should have waited," she snapped. "He wants to spend his life with you – he could wait a few days and do it properly."

"I think it was much better this way," I said. "We just got on with it."

"Well, it's wrong," she said, her arms folded and her mouth a thin line in her flushed face. "I don't agree with it."

"We're not in 1930 anymore, Mother," I said. "Things are different nowadays."

"That doesn't mean they're any better..."

I could see this conversation was going downhill fast. "Well, he proposed, I accepted, and we're getting married. So whatever you think, it's happening."

She stayed silent for a few moments. "When?" she demanded. "And where?"

"St Peter's in Eaton Square," I said. "On Saturday the eleventh of November."

"I see." She tapped her foot while staring at me, and I could virtually see the cogs going round. "I suppose you want me to make your wedding dress? And the bridesmaids' dresses?"

"That would be lovely," I replied, pleased I could give her a stake in the wedding. It may not have meant full acceptance by her, but at least it was something. "Then he's taking me to Paris," I added. "For the honeymoon."

"At least that's one thing he's doing right," she muttered, as she uncrossed her arms.

St Peter's Church stands on the corner of Eaton Square and Hobart Place in West London. It is one of the most magnificent and impressive churches in the area, which is why Barry's father and Cynthia thought it suitable for our wedding. Looking as if it has stepped straight out of Ancient Greece, it features a magnificent neo-classical frontage with a portico of six Ionic columns topped by a pitched fascia and finally a nod to the modern world; a tall clock tower.

Just like in Ancient Greece, St Peter's looks its best when set against a clear blue sky and bright sunshine. Sadly, on the eleventh of November 1961, this was not the backdrop. Instead, the skies were slate grey, and it pissed down with rain.

But I was pleased we had decided to get married, and was determined that the weather would not affect the event. Looking back, I think my main feeling was one of relief – that after a long time as a couple we were finally having the ceremony. And the icing on the (wedding) cake? At last, I could get out of my mother's place in Warwick Square and start to live my own life.

My father and mother were perfectly happy to let Barry's parents get on with it, preferring to stick with their allotted tasks. My mother was making the dresses, while my father was providing the cars. I was concerned he would turn up to collect me in one of his black and white Fiat Multipla taxis, but thankfully he'd found a white limousine from somewhere, so at least I arrived in a bit of style.

The dress my mother made was simple and elegant, and to give her her due, it did make me feel incredibly beautiful and very special. She used the classic A-line that had become the hallmark of bridal fashion at the time, and a high bateau neckline she 'borrowed' from Balenciaga (she said this was 'refined and demure'). There was no beading or embroidery apart from the silk edging on the floor-length hem; she wanted the soft-sheen duchess satin and classic cut to speak for itself. With short sleeves and a tulle veil, the whole effect was timelessly elegant.

The same cannot be said of the bridesmaids' dresses, which she made in dusty pink and gold, with ruffled necklines, lacy sleeves and mid-length voluminous skirts straight out of the 1950s. This meant that Charlotte, Ingrid and our cousin Susan looked somewhat frumpy next to my understated elegance – which I suspect was her aim all along.

The service went by in a bit of a whirl, with the actual marriage part seeming to come round almost immediately. There was a reading by Barry's father and a couple of hymns, and in no time at all we emerged onto the steps of St. Peter's to the cheers of our friends and lots of confetti being thrown over us. Much of it seemed to glue itself to my dress in the drizzle.

The reception was held at the 31 Room, and I have pictures of me and Barry posing with food platters direct from the kitchen, with Barry wearing an enormous chef's toque on his head as I pop some tasty piece of food in his mouth. This picture, as well as all the other main ones, was taken by Alex Stirling, who had agreed to be our official photographer. This meant we got fewer photos done than I wanted, as he spent ages arranging everyone, and refused to take the shot until every person was exactly where he wanted them. Now when I look at the photos, all I see is how everyone is standing with fixed 'rictus' grins in the rain, clearly wanting Alex to get on with it.

After the sit-down wedding breakfast, there were the speeches. These were made by the best man, who thankfully avoided anything too embarrassing, while the father-of-the-bride speech was made by some aged uncle whose name I forget.

He had stepped in at short notice, after my father decided he couldn't be bothered to give a speech. I had found this out on the morning of the wedding when Father had turned up with the car, and it soon became clear how unprepared – and apparently unconcerned – he was.

I had made some passing remark about him making sure his speech was both appropriate and not too long, when he shrugged and informed me, "I've decided not to speak at the reception."

"But you're the father of the bride," I said, aghast. "You must."

"Yes, well, I don't think I'll bother.

At this point I may have stamped my foot. "You're supposed to make a speech!"

"Come now, Annabelle," he replied, putting his hands in his pockets. "I was hardly around much when you were growing up. Whatever could I say?"

It was my wedding day, and he was – as ever – setting out to spoil things. "You could think of something!" I snapped. "This is your one chance to do something for your eldest daughter," I felt a prickle of tears starting. "As a loving father."

He gave a derisive snort. "I've arranged the car, haven't I?" He raised his chin and looked down his nose. "As the owner of London's leading taxi firm," he said in a self-important voice, "it's critical that my daughter is seen to arrive at the church in style." He dropped his head and fixed me with his eye. "Think how it would look if I didn't take care of that, Annabelle?"

"Better than not giving the father-of-the-bride speech," I said. If all he cared about was being seen to have procured a stupid car, then all hope was lost.

"And anyway," he added, pouring oil on the flames, "I'm here, aren't I? I think that should be enough."

So old Uncle Whoever was quickly pressed into service. Despite him knowing less about me than my own father, he managed to say some nice things and raise a few laughs. But to this day I cannot forgive Thomas Sylvester. I suppose he was one of those men who were not cut out for parenting (and in my eighty-plus years, I have seen a fair few of those), but to be so dismissive and self-absorbed on his daughter's special day was callous in the extreme. As a mother I have always tried to be there for my kids, and to create a warm, supportive environment for them. I suspect this is simply because I have experienced first-hand how devastating it is when a parent fails in this simple task.

※ ※

The day after the wedding, Mr and Mrs Barry Gregory headed off to Paris for their honeymoon. We had decided we would limit the trip to just three days; things were so busy at the 31 Room Barry felt unable to be away for too long.

But we certainly managed to cram a lot into the holiday, including dinner in a lovely restaurant with a friend of Barry's father, who had also given us the hotel room for our stay as a wedding gift. I don't recall much about the friend, or the meal, except that Barry kept staring at the waiters and passing comment on their skills – or lack of – with the silver service.

The event I do remember was our visit to Le Lido to see the Bluebell Girls.

Not only did we get to see the show for free, but we were also given Champagne and treated as the special guest of Miss Bluebell herself, Margaret Kelly.

This was down to us having met a man called Peter Baker at a party in London earlier in the year. It was another of the frenetic London parties, like the ones Jilly Norton threw, to which Barry and I were seemingly invited every weekend. The kind where the volume of music and conversation created the need to shout in order to be heard.

We were in the thick of the throng at this particular party, and Barry was in an animated shouted conversation with some rotund fellow about the restaurant business. Feeling a bit left out, I decided to get some more drinks. When I eventually managed to fight my way back to Barry, he was now talking to a dark-haired man with grey at his temples.

"Annabelle!" Barry yelled as I handed him a drink, "you must meet Peter Baker. He's London-based, but most of his work is securing dancers for the famous Bluebell Girls in Paris."

I raised an eyebrow. I had not heard of them.

"The Bluebell Girls perform at Le Lido on the Champs-Élysées," Peter Baker shouted. "It's a high-class cabaret and floor show. Very tasteful, mind." He gave me a 'significant' look that I felt merited a response.

"Are you suggesting I audition?" I asked. "I'm not a dancer."

Peter made a polite smile. "I'm sorry, Annabelle," he replied. "But you're also too short. Miss Bluebell has made it a rule that she will only employ girls over five foot nine."

I laughed. "Well there it is," I said. "I'm let off on two counts."

Barry said, "Peter's been telling me about Miss Bluebell. Apparently, she was originally with the Folies Bergère and known as 'Bluebell' because of her bright blue eyes. Then she created her own dance troupe, and now they are well established at Le Lido." He paused, as the music suddenly got very loud, then quietened again. "And it's a restaurant as well?" he asked Peter.

"Indeed it is, old boy," was the reply.

"It sounds fascinating," Barry said. "I'd like to learn more. Maybe there's something I can use in my own restaurant."

"You have a place yourself?" asked Peter.

"Yes, the 31 Room on Dover Street."

Peter's eyes opened wide. "Oh," he exclaimed, "I eat there all the time." He clapped Barry on the back. "It's the best, old boy. One of my favourites."

"Then your next meal is on me," yelled Barry. "And we can learn more about this cabaret." He paused for more loud music. "And be better able to hear each other, too!"

Barry was as good as his word, and a few nights later, Peter Baker was treated to a complimentary meal at the 31 Room. From this, the two of them became good friends, and we were assured that if we ever decided to visit Le Lido, we would get the same courtesy ourselves.

So on our honeymoon, when we presented ourselves at Le Lido, we were greeted by an elegant woman with a blonde perm; Miss Bluebell herself.

"Come in, darlings," she said in a broad Irish brogue. "Peter called ahead and said I was to give you the full experience, on the house."

We were sat at a table close to the stage, plied with Champagne, and treated to an unbelievable spectacle. There were canoes on water, performers skating on ice; and of course, the Bluebell Girls themselves. Tall beyond belief in their five-inch heels, beautifully cut corsets and feathered headdresses, they high-kicked, danced and pirouetted, all with smiles that never broke, even for an instant.

"Quite magnificent," Barry said, then patted my knee. "Don't you agree, Mrs Gregory?"

I sank into my seat with a contented sigh as the girls made the highest kick yet.

No longer Annabelle Sylvester. Now I was Mrs Gregory.

And it felt good.

My Portrait

This picture was taken while I was modelling for TV and press adverts (I don't recall who took it). But it was the look of the time, and it really took me back to my modelling days. There were so many ads, some of which I still have, and I may put up on my website.

Chapter Twelve

Becoming The Face of So Many Brands

Our return to London was a whirlwind of more parties, the approach of Christmas, and the thing I especially looked forward to – our move into the top floor flat at 105 Ebury Street.

My mother had tried to be magnanimous about me moving out of Warwick Square, but I could see it was quite an effort for her.

"It will be nice," she said through gritted teeth, as I pushed the last of my clothes into the suitcase and snapped the catches, "to have a place of your own."

"Yes," I agreed. She was right in a way, but it would be more than 'nice' to run a home my way. The way I wanted.

"You'll be back I expect, if you want me to run up a dress for you," she said, an air of satisfaction in her tone.

I gave a small shrug. "Perhaps." I pictured the couture number Cy Endfield had bought me hanging in my new wardrobe. "Although I am getting some lovely outfits as part of my modelling."

"And you prefer shop-bought gear to your own mother's hand-made?" Now she was using her 'wounded by heartless daughter' tone of voice.

I felt my blood rising. "I'm not playing this game, Mother," I snapped, trying – rather unsuccessfully – to avoid letting my annoyance show. "I don't want to be guilt-tripped by you." I took a breath. "I am grateful for all you have done, and the wedding dress was lovely. It made me feel very special. But I'm married now. I am going to live with Barry."

"That doesn't make it easier for a mother," she said. "Seeing the little girl she raised leaving her."

"I'm really not going to play this game," I repeated, deciding not to challenge her on how much 'raising' she had actually done. "Ebury Street is a short walk away. If you need me, I can be back." I winced inwardly; I did not want to be still at her beck and call. "But my life is with Barry now." I paused, considering whether I wanted to add another thing. I decided I would. "We're even thinking we'll start a family soon," I said, looking her straight in the eye. *May as well get it out in the open; she'll find out soon enough if it happens.*

She gave a small, derisive snort. "You're only twenty," she observed. "I was much older when you came along."

I refrained from pointing out that this could be part of the reason why she'd been such a distant mother. "There's no guarantee I'll get pregnant immediately. And anyway," I added, "I've got lots more ads lined up. They seem to like me as a model, and my schedule's looking pretty full for the next year."

This was true; there were several more Player's ads in the pipeline, most of which would feature me and Colin, although not all would be directed by Cy Endfield. While Colin and I seemed to be lining up as the faces of the brand, Cy was becoming more involved in a film project he'd been working on for a couple of years called *Zulu*. He'd been telling me and Colin all about it in Saint-Tropez. "It's set in South Africa in 1879," he had said. We were having a drink in a bar overlooking the harbour after the Player's filming had wrapped for the day. "It's about the battle of Rorke's Drift. A small, plucky group of Brits defend a garrison from attack by a large Zulu force. Stan Baker's up for it, and we've got a new young actor called Michael Caine slated for the Lieutenant Bromhead role." Colin and I were entranced; the world of film seemed so glamorous. "The funny thing is," Cy went on, "I was originally going to have him read for the part of a cockney corporal because that's his normal speaking voice. But as an American, I thought that's not what he actually *looked* like. To me he had the appearance of one of your English upper classes. So I asked if he could do 'posh'." Cy took a sip of wine. "Turns out he could."

Colin and I gave each other a knowing look. Even though my modelling career had only been a few days at that point, I already knew that if an actor is asked if they can do something, the answer is always 'yes', whether they can or not. Although, as Cy said, Michael Caine really could 'do posh'. He was excellent in the role, as I found out a few years later when Barry and I sat together in the darkened cinema watching the drama of Rorke's Drift unfold.

My mother gave another snort. "Advertising cigarettes. What kind of job is that, parading about smoking?"

"It's a good one," I said. "And it pays well, as it sells the product." This was true; my fee for the Player's ad was more money than I'd ever earned at Bermans, or anywhere else for that matter. In fact, the amount of money I eventually earned across my modelling career was almost embarrassing. Not only did it enable me to afford my true passion, creating art, but it also gave our family a lifestyle Barry's restaurant income – and subsequent antiques trading – could never have done.

Along with Player's, I ended up doing ads for Lifebuoy soap, including one where I was the girl who wouldn't go out with the boy because (whisper it in confidence), he had *body odour*. Indeed, the abbreviation 'BO' was made so ubiquitous by the Lifebuoy ads, that it became a part of the language – something I could perhaps be proud to have played my part in (or perhaps not...). Suffice to say, that once the lad had bathed himself with Lifebuoy, I was all over him.

I also did several ads for Kellogg's, as well as one for Cadbury's Fruit & Nut. The campaign featured someone apparently sensible, in contrast to someone else being a bit of a 'nut case'. In each one, the 'sensible' person watches the other being 'nutty', eats a Fruit & Nut bar, then does something equally 'nutty' themselves (what was in those bars?). The agency, which I think was the one called J. Walter Thomson, showed me the idea with an existing ad. It featured a 'sensible' man in a bowler hat. He watches a bunch of people cramming themselves into a phone booth, then eats the chocolate and runs away in a random 'nutty' way (speeded up to make it look even more odd).

"Can you do a cartwheel?" they asked me.

"Yes," I said, hoping they wouldn't ask me to demonstrate there and then (the room was too small). I figured I'd have time to learn how – if I got the job. Which fortunately I did. The ad featured a 'wacky' conceptual artist throwing paint at his canvas, while I was the girl watching through the window, eating the chocolate bar. I then went away doing speeded-up 'nutty' cartwheels.

The ad was shot on a riverside path – I think it was in Shepperton – and they kept making me retake the cartwheels. "Your legs aren't high enough," the director said each time. "Let's go again." By the time my palms were scraped raw, and I was heartily sick of it, the J. Walter Thomson producer said, "Actually, I think that last one was OK. It's quite 'nutty' if she's not doing perfect cartwheels. And anyway," he added, "she runs round the lamppost like a kid. I think that's 'nutty' enough."

Another series of ads I did was for a Wall's ice cream lolly called Top Ten. This involved me eating the product in several close-up shots, then holding it up while I did a skiffle dance across the frame, grinning like a fool. Which was fine in principle, but in practice, not so easy. Have you ever eaten a large mouthful of ice cream, while smiling inanely, trying not to get brain freeze, and looking like it's the best thing you've ever tasted? Let me tell you, it's not as easy as it looks. I feel I was worth every penny they paid me for that ad.

There were plenty more TV ads, including ones for brands such as Palmolive and Stork Margarine. I wanted to see them again recently – not only as research for this memoir but also for old times' sake. However, it seems – despite my friends doing some extensive searches on the internet – most of them no longer exist. Which is probably just as well.

Then there were photoshoots where all I had to do was pose for a static shot, holding some product or other and either smiling or looking sultry. One of these was Johnson's Baby Cream. Wearing only a skimpy lace-topped slip, I had my hand on my cheek (had I just applied the product? I suppose I must have done). The copy says, 'Not just for baby... a pure gentle facial moisturiser.' For some reason I'm looking quite worried. Was I concerned the product wouldn't work? Who knows.

Another one in the late 1960s, I remember, was for Barclaycard. This was around the time when charge or credit cards were starting to come in. The problem was retailers seemed to struggle with all the bother they had to go to, in order to make a credit card sale. That's because it *was* so much bother! First you had to fit the embossed card into the imprinter (often called the 'click-clack machine' because of the noise they made), then lay the carbon-copy slip over the top and pull the handle across and back, all while hoping the slip would stay in place. And if that went OK, you still had to check that the embossed information from the card had come through on every part of the slip. So much to do! Even I, a lady of advanced years, can see that the modern thing where you just wave your card at the machine is so much better.

It seemed at the time that the clever marketing people at Barclaycard had given the complexity of the process much thought. They had decided that the best way to force retailers to go to the bother of taking card payment was to have the customer demand it. Which in turn, meant having a sultry looking young woman telling them to. So I was photographed looking deeply pensive, with my chin on my hand. The resulting picture was mounted on cardboard and cut out, then stood on pretty much every shop counter in the country. It must have worked, as we now seem to buy everything with a card. Although to be fair, my real preference is still for cash.

At the time, this campaign was something my mother could not accept. "Every shop I go into, Annabelle," she complained, "I have you staring at me. How can I concentrate on my shopping when your eyes keep following me as I walk around? Everywhere I go!"

"All I did was pose for the shot," I replied. "What they choose to do with it afterwards is none of my business." Then I added, "Once I've been paid, of course."

"You mean they pay you for all this standing around and holding up products?" she asked, with a look of mock surprise. "And behaving like a fool after eating a bar of chocolate?"

"Yes, Mother," I said with a sigh. "Of course they do."

She shook her head. "It is hardly a proper job. Why don't you do something worthwhile?" She raised her eyebrow. "Like dressmaking?"

I shook my head. "This is a proper job. One most girls would be desperate to get." She didn't look convinced, so I added, "I would have thought a mother would be proud of a daughter who's achieved so much."

She gave a derisive snort. "If you call it an achievement. Pouting for a camera."

I took a breath to calm my rising temper. "It *is* an achievement, Mother. It's a career."

"If you say so."

I could see there was no point in continuing this conversation, so I ended it there. But it did upset me. As I had said, most mothers would have been delighted for their daughter getting regular modelling work, but not mine.

Did Twiggy or Jean Shrimpton have similar conversations with their mothers? I doubted it.

Despite her lack of support, I managed to keep my modelling career going throughout the 1960s, despite (or maybe because of) becoming a mother myself. Marcus came along in 1963, Wayne in 1964, and Sacha in 1968.

And all this while Barry was building his own career in the restaurant and nightclub trade. It was a career that involved very long hours each day, which meant that our time together was becoming increasingly rare.

'Barry on the Sofa'

Conté crayon

One of the rare moments when Barry was relaxing at home, so I took the opportunity to dash off this quick portrait sketch.

Chapter Thirteen

Becoming The Boss's Wife

Running the 31 Room was an all-consuming job. Barry would get home at around 2 a.m., then leave to go back to the restaurant at around 10 a.m. Meanwhile, I was running out to shoots – both for still photos and for TV ads. Often there were days when we never saw each other; he must have crawled into bed when I was asleep, and I would then get up for an early call before he had surfaced.

There were a few brief meetings of course; when I didn't have a shoot, or on Sundays when the restaurant was closed. And at breakfast on one such occasion, my frustration had built to a point where it just had to burst.

He had his nose buried in his newspaper, and it was as if I was invisible. I had made us both a cup of tea, and it was when I slammed his mug down with a little too much force and slopped hot tea onto the table, that I finally seemed to have his attention. He lowered his paper with an enquiring frown. "What is it, Annabelle?" he asked, then added with typical male insensitivity, "is something the matter, love?"

"Yes," I growled as I dropped onto my chair. I waited for him to say something; to show he understood the problem. But his frown morphed into a look of mute enquiry, making it clear he wasn't going to respond. Or didn't understand.

The silence continued until I could bear it no longer. "You must know what it is, Barry," I said. "We never see each other."

There was another long pause while he seemed to consider this. "Yes, we do," he said, with the kind of sickly smile adults give to a wayward child. "We're seeing each other now, aren't we?"

"Oh come on," I snapped. "It's a pretty rare event, and anyway, you're reading the paper not talking to me."

"I do need to know what's going on in the world," he said, tapping it.

"And you spend all day in that restaurant."

"It's my work, Annabelle," he replied. "I have mine, and you have yours."

I was beginning to find his calm pragmatism even more annoying than his silence.

"But you're there every night until the small hours," I snapped, then I groaned inwardly; it was a hollow point. Sure enough, he came straight back.

"We have a late music licence, as you know. It makes us pretty unique." He lifted the paper slightly and his eyes started sliding down towards it. I gave him a warning growl, and his attention came back to me. "It means we can operate almost as a nightclub, and that's where the money is."

"But that doesn't mean you need to be there every hour," I countered.

"It does actually." The top of his paper dropped back towards the table. "I am the face of the 31 Room. I don't just meet and greet; I make our VIP guests feel at ease. I make them feel so welcome that they come back and spend even more money."

"And these 'VIP's are more 'very important people' than your wife?" I said, unable to keep the note of triumph out of my voice. That was a killer comment. "They clearly see you a lot more than I do."

"We had Bobby Butlin in three times in the last month," he announced with a look of quiet satisfaction, as if this alone proved his point. "And we had Diz Disley playing his music the other night. The place was rammed."

"Great," I said, "a holiday park owner's son and a guitarist. Hardly the big league."

He got up and went to the sink. "Billy Smart was in recently," he said, turning back to me with a small smile. As if that was the clincher.

"Oh," I said, faking surprise. "Did he bring his circus elephants?"

Barry tut-tutted. "Come now, love. It's a good business and it's bringing in money." He picked up a cloth and came back to the table. "You should come in more often," he said, lifting his mug and wiping up the tea ring. "It's like a party in there every night, and I know how much you love a party."

I sat back and regarded him over my mug. *Maybe I should go in more often*, I thought. *Be seen as the boss's wife*. "OK," I said. "I'll come in tonight."

⁂

That night I dressed carefully, putting on the French dress Cy had bought and curling my hair into 'The Flip'. I even put on a bit of make-up.

There was no sign of Barry when I went in; it was Tony, the Head Waiter who gave me a seat at the bar. I ordered a Dry Martini, then swivelled on my stool, crossed my legs and took a long look around.

The 31 Room was on two floors; the upper being a mezzanine with a balcony that looked down to the main bar where I sat. There were plenty of diners on both levels, as waiters moved with effortless ease between the tables, balancing seemingly impossible numbers of dishes in their hands.

The diners and drinkers themselves all seemed extremely well-heeled; there was plenty of money in the room, and faces

I recognised from the world of TV, film and stage. They all seemed to be drinking to excess, and there was lots of shouting, name-calling and raucous behaviour, although it never seemed to get out of hand. As I looked around, I couldn't help thinking that these were people who didn't need to worry where the next hundred pounds – or even thousand – was coming from, and probably didn't have the same concerns as the rest of us more 'normal' people.

With a sigh, I looked over to my left and made a small frown. There was another bar with the curious name, 'The Clown Bar'. I knew there was a second, more intimate bar room, but I didn't recall ever seeing that name there before.

Beyond the entrance to the Clown Bar there was a display cabinet, side-on to where I sat, containing something both strange and totally unexpected. It was several rows of hard-boiled eggs on glass shelves. Each one was sitting on a little black plinth, and they were all painted with colourful faces.

Clutching my glass, I slid off my bar stool and went in, stopping in front of the cabinet for a closer look. I was greeted by row after row of tiny clown faces, staring at me like a miniature circus. They were all painted in such detail it was as if the real performers were looking back at me. Some had hats – such as trilbies, toppers and conical Pierrots. Most had hair added in a variety of colours and styles, and there were a range of red noses, sad and happy mouths, and garish eyes.

I studied them more closely. The artists who had done the painting were clearly very technical, and had a good knowledge of creating real-looking faces. Some of the eggs had eyes that were almost photographic. It was not my style of painting, but I was impressed by the skill and dedication it must have taken.

Under each one was a name on a small card, presumably of the owner of the face. Joey the Clown, for example, had a full white make-up with a red tip painted on his nose, while Lou Jacobs had massive white eyebrows, a raised bald headpiece, and tufts of wispy ginger hair above his ears. His nose was covered by a stuck-on red ball. Another clown was called Sir Robert Fossett. He had black make-up that snaked down his white cheeks from the outer edges of his eyes. There were also three black droplet shapes in the centre of his forehead, giving good symmetry.

My examination of these remarkable items was interrupted by Barry, joining me at the cabinet. "Hi, Annabelle," he said. "You came in, then?" It wasn't really a question – more an observation.

"Yes, Barry," I replied, before tearing my eyes away from the display and looking up at him. Was there still a small frisson left over from the argument that morning? Barry's expression seemed to suggest not as far as he was concerned. I felt my eyes narrow as I tried to work out if we were OK now. After all, I had said a few unkind things. Was he prepared to let them go? Or had he simply forgotten them?

"That's nice," he said. "Lovely to see you in here." On balance, and knowing him, he had probably forgotten. "Do you like the new display?" he asked, indicating the painted eggs.

"It's certainly very impressive," I replied, then gave him a curious stare. "What on earth is it?"

He laughed. "It's clown copyright. Every circus clown has their own individual make-up look, and they want to protect it from being copied – either deliberately or by accident. It's painted on an egg and put on display, for 'the record' so to speak. There's no specific legal way to protect a clown-face copyright, so it's done like this."

"I see," I said, nodding slowly as I took this in. It seemed to make sense, except for two things. "How did you come by this display?" Then I added, "And, more importantly, why is it here?"

Again he laughed. "My inquisitive Annabelle," he said. "The collection was originally created by a chemist called Stan Bult. He's very old now, but he's been in a few times, and told me about his eggs. Painting them was originally a hobby of his, but now the clowns themselves have adopted the idea. I said it sounded fascinating, and they would make a great talking point for the restaurant, so he agreed to loan me the collection. We've put them in here and renamed it 'The Clown Bar'."

"Gosh," I said. "You'd better look after them."

"Sure will," he said, with his boyish grin. I found myself grinning back. He clearly had moved on from the argument that morning.

Seemed like I had better do the same.

I went into the restaurant more regularly after that. Not only did it get me out of the flat in the evenings, but it also meant I could spend more time with my husband. I even took to coming in two or three times a week, where I sat at the bar, drank Dry Martinis, and chatted with the patrons.

While this meant I felt a lot better about us being together, I did have one particular thing I still found upsetting – and it was as much my own fault than anything Barry was doing.

My art.

In the years since I had left St Martin's, I had tried to draw or paint every day. This could have been anything from some sketching when I found the time, to attending a life class, to working on a painting. It was as if I had an art addiction and needed my daily 'fix'.

But once we were married and living in the Ebury Street flat, I seemed to lose both the time and the inclination. Days were spent at shoots, while evenings were either going to the 31 Room, learning scripts or attending meetings with photographers and directors. Over time, I found my art sessions were getting fewer and fewer.

I spoke to Barry about it one evening in the restaurant.

"Don't worry, love," he said when I had poured out my woes. "I'm sure you'll find time soon."

"When, Barry?" I asked. "I'm working every day, and in the evenings I don't have the time, or frankly the mental energy, to draw or paint."

"Then that's your mind's way of saying you need a break from it," he said, with the air of one who has now solved an otherwise intractable problem.

"Not at all," I said. "My mind is quite clear I want to, but I can't see how to fit it into my life. It's... it's..." I sought the best way to put it. "It's as if something inside me has died."

I didn't know it at the time, but in fact the opposite was true. Something inside me was very much alive – and starting to grow.

Dancing Nightly

to the

Art Fairbank Trio

Fully licensed until 3.0 a.m.

Open from 12 noon — 2.30 p.m.   7.0 p.m. — 2.0 a.m.

The 31 Room Card

The 31 Room was one of the only restaurants in London's West End with a music licence, which made it as much a nightclub as a restaurant. Finding this card in an album brought back one of the strangest events that happened there.

Chapter Fourteen

Becoming A Mother

Marcus Gregory was born in March 1963.

I had only been able to work up until the second trimester, before my baby bump started to become very obvious. Once Marcus came along, my priorities changed; looking after this little bundle was all I cared about. He was an easy infant, sleeping through the night from fairly early on and being generally quite relaxed. Which was more than I could say for myself; I was terrified of my responsibility as a new mother and paranoid about keeping the flat and everything around the baby totally spotless and hygienic.

Barry seemed bemused by my concerns. "A few germs are necessary," he observed one morning, as I was busy boiling the baby blankets.

"I can't take the risk," I muttered, stirring the cloth in the bubbling water. "If I don't do it properly, some ghastly bug could kill him."

"Now you're just being silly," Barry said. "Look at him." He pointed to where Marcus was lying in his crib, gurgling away with a smile. "The boy's as strong as an ox."

"Well, I'm not taking chances," I replied.

"You should," he said. "If the child doesn't get exposed to nasty things early, how is he going to build up his immunity?"

I raised an eyebrow. "Nasty things that might kill him first, you mean?"

Barry gave a small sigh. "Of course not, Annabelle," he said. "But you can't wrap him in a blanket all his life." Then he added in a strangely flat voice, "He's going to need to fight back when things threaten him."

I gave the cloth another stir. Of course, he had a point. Marcus would need to be protected from things that could harm him. But right now, as his mother, I wanted to preserve the hygienic bubble around my baby for as long as possible. "I suppose..." I began, looking up. There was such a strange, wide-eyed look on Barry's face, that the words froze in my mouth. This was not about Marcus any more. It was about Barry himself. He was in trouble.

"Barry," I said slowly. "Is something wrong?" I swallowed hard. "Is someone threatening you?"

He gave me a level stare. "They did, yes."

My hand flinched, causing the wooden spoon to fall into the boiling water. I left it. "Who, Barry?" I whispered.

"Have you heard of the Kray brothers, Ronnie and Reggie?"

I shook my head.

"They're a couple of gangsters who pretty much run the East End." He paused. "They paid us a visit last night."

"Oh no!" I exclaimed. *Gangsters!* "What did they want?" I turned the gas down so the pot wouldn't boil over.

His face darkened. "It's well known that they demand protection money from businesses in the East End."

"Protection?" I asked. "From what?"

"From what they'll do if you don't pay up."

"Did they demand money from you?" I whispered. I knew that occasionally some dodgy people came into the restaurant, but actual gangsters? That was another level.

"They did. And I told them to fuck off." I must have gone white, as he added, "It was the right thing to do, Annabelle. I told them they were off their patch; that there was no way they could pull that kind of stunt in Mayfair. I said that if they didn't go immediately, I would call the police."

"And did you?" I asked, still trying to get my head round all this.

"Yes, when they went up to the mezzanine balcony, and started throwing glasses, crockery and even tables and chairs down to the floor below, I managed to get a call in to the police, who came pretty quickly." His face went even darker. "Even so, there was a fair bit of damage done before the police arrived and got the brothers out."

He looked as if that was all there was to it. But I could see there was more.

"But you said they were gangsters, Barry," I pointed out. "And people like that have guns and bats and things." I must have heard that somewhere – maybe from Cy or Alex Stirling. "And you swore at them and called the police. They could have killed you. They could come back!" I gasped. Marcus would lose his father, and I would become a single mother.

"No." His face brightened slightly. "The police have got tabs on them now, and if anything happened to me, the Krays would be in the frame for sure. I don't think they'd try it on; it's not like I'm some East End rival. So if I was attacked, they'd swing for sure."

"But Barry, this is horrible," I exclaimed. Gangsters throwing glasses and tables down from the balcony! "Oh no!" I put a hand to my mouth. "Is the restaurant ruined?"

"There's a fair bit of damage," he admitted. "We're going to have to close for a few days until we can sort it out."

"That's dreadful!" I gasped, as another thought hit me. "And the eggs?" I asked. "The clowns?"

His usual grin returned. "Yeah, they're OK. All still clowning."

༺༻

Barry was right; the Krays never did come back, and the 31 Room was left alone. We restored the restaurant to order, and things returned to normal. Or at least, normal for Barry. I was still struggling to manage being effectively trapped in the flat with the baby while he carried on living his life pretty much as it was before. I say 'pretty much' – he did what he could, even though it was little compared to my responsibilities.

My mother came round one day; ostensibly to offer help, but I think more probably to check up on how I was managing as a mother myself. And to give me the benefit of her wisdom. She had now got a job with the Christian Dior couture salon in Conduit Street, with the honorific title of 'Madame'. This made her think her opinion on all matters – not just fashion, but babies as well – was as important outside the salon as it was inside.

Even though it was her day off, she was dressed for work and swept into the flat looking like she was about to manage some high-end client's dress fitting. From her charcoal Dior tailored suit with its cinched waist and mid-length skirt, to her polished blue court shoes, neat chignon, pill-box hat and perfectly applied rose lipstick, she was every inch Dior's 'Madame'.

"And you say this husband of yours is working all hours?" she asked, once she had carefully removed a baby blanket and perched, with her knees locked together, on the front of our G Plan easy chair. "When does he help with the baby?"

"He helps," I said, ever the loyal wife.

"But he is out all day and all night. How?"

I had my back to her at that moment, pouring the tea from the pot. I considered my reply carefully before turning. "He takes the baby out in the pram on a Sunday morning, so I get a lie-in. And he spends an hour playing with Marcus every morning."

The corner of her mouth turned up. "It seems fairly little to me. Compared to how much you must do."

"I don't seem to recall Father being much help with us," I pointed out, handing her a cup of tea. "At least Barry isn't running off with a succession of floozies."

"You're always telling me this is the sixties," she said, seeming to avoid the question. "Men should be more helpful with their families. Your father was from an older generation."

"Hardly an excuse for the way he behaved," I observed. "He wouldn't even make a speech at my wedding."

She ignored this. "Your Barry should do more." Her voice took on a deeply disapproving tone. "He leaves it all to you, Annabelle."

Marcus began to grizzle. "I just get on with it," I said, as I picked him out of his crib and calmed him with the dummy. "I always make the best of things."

"But you don't go out?" she asked.

"Of course," I replied, bouncing Marcus on my lap. "I take him out in the pram myself at least once a day, when I pick things up from the shops."

Marcus held a chubby arm out towards her. "He wants to have a cuddle with his grandma," I suggested.

She glanced down at her wool crepe lap, then back at me with a look of mild panic. "I don't think so."

When she'd gone, I put Marcus back down in his crib. As he looked up at me with his bright blue eyes, I sighed. "Your grandfather didn't seem to be bothered with me, let alone you," I said. "And your grandmother was more concerned about keeping her skirt pristine than giving you a hug." I put a finger into his hand, and he gripped it tight. "You are going to be part of a warm loving family, Marcus," I said. "Your father and I, we love you. We will always be there for you."

LORDS 28 Finchley Road, N.W.8.

Telephone: 01-722 4425

Dear

At last, after six months of rebuilding and decorating we are now ready to open 'Lords', and have fixed the date for the 4th of July. The club is situated at 28 Finchley Road, just past St. John's Wood Tube Station, and surprisingly only about five minutes from Oxford St., and with no parking problems. At present, the club will be closing at Midnight, but from September we will be open till 2 a.m.

The Club consists of an Oak panelled restaurant seating forty, and serving English and Continental food at moderate prices. The unusual bar includes a dance floor, and in contrast to the restaurant is rather more with-it in design. Incidentally, we will not be deafening our members with the worst half of the Hit Parade, and will even encourage "contact" dancing.

In opening Lords we have tried to create a club with interesting decor and a good atmosphere, where one can go for a drink, or a meal and a dance, dressed formally or informally and know that it will not end up costing a fortune. We are sure that once you have paid us a visit, most of you will want to call again.

Hope to see you soon,

R. B. Gregory   A. B. Hung   C. C. Gregory

The Lords Club

This letter fell out of an album while I was browsing through, transporting me back to Barry's next venture. Incidentally, he might have promised not to deafen his patrons with the worst of the Hit Parade, but that didn't mean they kept the music quiet!

Chapter Fifteen

Becoming The Girl About Town

In 1964, a year after Marcus was born, Barry decided to sell the 31 Room.

"I think it has run its course," he told me. "It's a restaurant trying to be a nightclub – it's neither one thing nor the other."

"What will you do?" I asked, supporting myself with a hand on the side of the table, as the new baby gave a kick inside my womb.

"I met this guy who wants to open a place on the Finchley Road," he said. "So we'll be going into business together. Clive's in as well. We're thinking of calling it the Lords Club."

"Sounds interesting," I said, wincing as a tiny heel thumped into my diaphragm.

This second pregnancy had come so soon after the first, that my attempt to restart my modelling career had been cut short almost before it had begun. I had found an agency in Welbeck Street that provided nannies and baby-sitters, so I was able to get back to work once Marcus could be left under their care. I'd got an ad – I forget what product it was for – and it was directed by the lovely Dick Lester. He was a very kind and generous man; a softly spoken American. Dick was more used to shooting feature films, and it seemed he wanted me for a part in his next project, *A Hard Day's Night* with The Beatles.

"A lot of the early sequences are set on a train," he told me in a break from filming the ad. "I see you in the role of Jean. It's a small part; she's one of the young girls on the train who meets the lads from the band, but she needs to be a good actress and visually memorable. I think you'd be great in the role."

I was speechless. To be in a film... and with The Beatles... "I'd love to," I managed eventually, already imagining how my career would take off. "When does shooting start?"

"Early March. Will you be available?"

"Of course," I said, then stopped. I knew I was pregnant again, and by March I'd be five months, so there was every chance I'd be showing.

I cautiously told him this, and he shook his head. "Sorry, Annabelle," he said. "Jean is young; she's a schoolgirl. There's no way she could have a baby bump."

In the end, he cast Pattie Boyd, another model I had met occasionally at photo shoots. As a result of meeting George Harrison on the film – and subsequently marrying him – her modelling career moved into the stratosphere. She even ended up marrying Eric Clapton after divorcing George.

So if the new baby hadn't come along, who knows what direction my career might have taken?

But... it didn't go anywhere, as Wayne Gregory arrived in July 1964. Once again, I was a captive mum, although by then we were in a lovely semi-detached house in Goldhurst Terrace, so my captivity was not quite as difficult to endure as it had been in the Ebury Street top-floor flat. There was more room for Marcus to play, and a garden where we could sit out in the sunshine.

Barry's new club started to take off. Once Wayne had arrived and was a few months old, I was able to get out (with the help of the baby-sitting agency) and join Barry for one or two evenings a week.

If the 31 Room was a place for the rich and entitled, the Lords Club soon became the centre of a social set that loved to party – and, like everyone in those days – to smoke. Every time I went there I felt as if I stank of cigarettes. I couldn't wait to jump in the bath and wash my hair when I got home.

The bar was one of the defining features of the club. Barry's idea had been to get hold of a number of old upright pianos, then line them up to form the bar. Each piano had all the hammers and strings removed to make the space for an internal shelf – while the keys themselves were left intact. Patrons could then sit up at the bar and run their hands over the keys while they waited for their drink.

Another feature was the furniture, which was all made of cardboard; something very avant-garde in the 1960s. I was concerned it would be a problem, given it was in an environment where there were both drinks and drunks. Not a good mix with cardboard.

"Not an issue, really," Barry said when I asked. "We have to replace each chair every few weeks, and each table every couple of months. But it's not expensive, and it's a great talking point."

Talking was something that happened a lot in the club, and very loudly too. This – along with the belting music – meant the volume was excessive, and one could hardly hear oneself think, let alone hold a realistically meaningful conversation. Just like the parties we had been going to before the kids had come along, you had to nod, smile, and try to make the person you were talking to think you'd heard what they'd said. Equally, you'd reply with a comment of your own, in the almost certain knowledge they wouldn't hear a word and were just nodding along politely themselves.

But if it was loud for people in the club, at least they had paid to get in and were prepared to accept the noise. The same cannot be said for the folk in the flat above, who had to endure the din night after night into the small hours. They were Diana Rigg, the actress, and her partner, the film director Philip Saville. I lost count of the times I saw this angry young woman in a silk housecoat and pyjamas barge her way in and storm up to the bar, demanding the noise was turned down.

Frankly, I admired her guts; it must have taken a lot to come down, push through the smoky room full of tightly packed bodies and make her complaint. Especially as the noise was never lowered by a single decibel.

I remember being at the bar one night, when she appeared beside me, and screamed something at the barman. I took it she was yelling, "Turn the sodding music down!" but I have never been much of a lip-reader. She then turned to me, as if looking for the solidarity of young women, and added something which I think may have been, "I've got a sodding audition tomorrow!"

In true Lords Club tradition, I nodded, smiled, and replied, "Oh yes. The weather's lovely this time of year, isn't it?"

She nodded, yelled what I suspected was, "Exactly!" and stormed back out of the club.

༺❦༻

The Lords Club was the centre of our lives for four or five years. And not just Barry's, but mine too. Looking back, I think going there kept me sane, stopping me from going stir-crazy in the house with the babies, and keeping me in touch with the life I had led before. I could put on a smart outfit, add a bit of make-up, do my hair, and for a few short hours, I was no longer the hassled mother but the social butterfly once more spreading her wings. Bear in mind, I was only twenty-three when I had Wayne. To be that age, and looking after two tiny boys, meant the urge to get a break from being a mum was very strong.

My third child, Sacha, didn't arrive until 1968, which was around the time when Barry and his partner fell out, and the club closed down. But up to that point it was a place to meet many of the up-and-coming personalities from the worlds of TV and music.

I was sitting up at the bar one evening, when a suave, elegant man in his mid-thirties, with dark hair and heavy eyebrows, came up to order a drink. Thankfully, at that time the club was less full than usual, and there was no music playing. So, when he leant on the top of one of the bar pianos and casually began a conversation, it was actually possible to hear what he was saying.

I had just ordered a Dry Martini, when the man said to the barman, "Tell her this drink is on me." He paused a beat, then added with perfect comic timing, "Unless of course, she's dangerously expensive."

I exchanged a quick glance with the barman, who knew perfectly well who I was, and indicated with a tiny nod that I was going to play along. "I hope you don't mind," the man continued. "I've got a terrible habit of buying drinks for women I've never met." Another comic pause, then the punchline, "Because the ones I do know all say no." He leaned across and gave me a perfect smile. "I'm Bob, by the way. Bob Monkhouse. Don't let the name put you off; my parents were hoping for a solicitor."

"Good evening, Mr Monkhouse," I said with a smile of my own. "Annabelle."

"Bob, please."

"I've seen you on *The Golden Shot*," I said.

"That's me. Weekends I try to help members of the public direct a blindfolded man to fire a crossbow, while on week nights, I try to impress intelligent women with cheap gags."

I shrugged. "You've got one out of the two."

"Ouch. If I'd known you were that quick, I would have spent more time writing the gags."

"Maybe better luck next time," I said, sliding off the stool and putting my arm around Barry as he came up. "My husband," I informed Bob. "He owns the club."

Bob gave a smooth smile. "That's good. I was worried he'd come to repossess my punchline."

He took the drink the barman had put on top of the piano for him. "Mr Gregory, I believe?" Barry nodded. "And your charming wife, Annabelle." He took a sip. "By way of apology for my behaviour, I would like to invite you both to come and see *The Golden Shot* being filmed. It's live on a Sunday afternoon."

"Thank you," Barry replied. "But Sunday's our only day off and we have two small children."

"Quite right." Bob gave Barry a game-show-host smile. "I wouldn't go either, but for some reason they pay me to be there."

Another person who used to come in was Des O'Connor, an all-round entertainer who had his own show where he sang songs, told jokes and interviewed other personalities. I once asked him if he was ever going to release a hit single.

"As it happens, I might be soon," he said, giving me his trademark cheeky smile. "I was recording a jingle at a studio in Highbury recently and bumped into the writer Les Reed. He said he'd just been recording with Quincy Jones, and that prompted me to ask him to write something for me. Les and his partner, Barry Mason, have written me a great number. I think it's going to be a hit."

"What's it called?" I asked. "I'll look out for it."

"'I Pretend'," he told me. "Geoff Love has done the arrangement."

Throughout this, I nodded wisely as he dropped each name, as if I knew who all these people were.

Barry asked me later what we'd been talking about, and I told him about the record. "He's too 'easy listening' for me,"

Barry observed. "I prefer something with a bit more bite. The Beatles' new album, *Sgt. Pepper*, for example. That's more my kind of thing."

'I Pretend' came out the following year, and I agreed with Barry; it was a bit too 'easy listening', although fairly pleasant. It even got to number one in the charts, so it must have had something about it.

The famous people we met were not just those who visited the club, but also those who had Barry do their catering. He did a fair few events that I forget now, but the one I do remember – for its over-the-top flamboyance – was for the pianist and entertainer, Liberace.

It was 1969, and John Rimington, the publicist who handled Liberace's affairs in London, was in the club one evening. He came up to Barry and me while we were at the bar.

"Barry, love," he said, "Word is, you do catering for parties. That right?"

"We do," Barry replied with a nod. "Do you have something coming up?"

"Absolutely." John took a sip of his daiquiri. "My chap Liberace is over at the moment, filming some television specials, and his sainted mum Frances is here as well. The thing is, he wants to throw her a party. But not just any party, something truly memorable. So I suggested Madame Tussauds, and he was all over it."

"Sounds fun," Barry agreed.

"Yes, well, apparently they've got a waxwork of him playing the piano, so he thinks it will be such a hoot to have the party there."

"Have you booked it?"

"Oh yes, love. It's all arranged for six weeks' time. All we need is the caterer. You in?"

"Sure."

"Excellent!" John gave Barry his card. "Call me in the morning and we'll sort out the details. I'm sure you'll do Liberace and Frances proud on the night." He glanced at me. "And your lovely wife can come along as a guest, naturally."

On the night, after we'd made sure the children were in bed and the babysitter was settled in, Barry and I got a taxi to Madame Tussauds. He'd come home briefly to shower and change after setting up all day, and now we could make our grand entrance; he in his immaculate white dinner jacket and me in a bold Yves St. Laurent Mondrian dress. Its shift silhouette, geometric designs and primary colours suited my mood that night: fun and daring.

As we were shown into the hall of celebrities, I was taken aback by the number of people already there. The room was buzzing, with white jacketed waiters moving around giving out glasses of Champagne or refilling empty ones. Tony, the barman originally from the 31 Room, came up and gave us our drinks.

"All good, Tony?" Barry asked.

"Yes, Mr Gregory."

John Rimington came up. "Barry, love," he said. "Great party! Frances is in heaven, and Liberace couldn't be more pleased. He wants to meet you to say thanks."

"Delighted," Barry said, shooting his cuffs. John's eyes widened as he spotted Barry's cufflinks.

"What are those?" he asked. "They look like tiny pistols."

"They are," Barry told him.

"They really fire?"

"Yes. But they wouldn't do any harm."

"Better keep that to yourself, love," John said, as he moved away.

I spotted Liberace through the crowds. He was sitting at his piano in a tasselled rhinestone jacket. A large candelabra was shining on top of the instrument, illuminating his broad smile as he played.

I nudged Barry. "There he is. Should we go up and introduce ourselves?"

"I wouldn't if I were you," Barry replied. "That's his waxwork."

If we had many well-known people of the time at the Lords Club, we got even more at Barry's next venture. This was called the Cine & Arts Club. It was in Greek Street, above where, a few years before, Peter Cook and Dudley Moore's Establishment Club had been. Not only did Barry's new place seem to attract famous people from the worlds of film, TV and music, but it also drew in a different type of 'celebrity'.

Members of the criminal underworld.

'Frankie'

Collage. 70cm x 64cm.

Frankie was the barmaid at the Cine & Arts Club and knew everything about everyone who came in. We got on well, and she came over to our house at Goldhurst Terrace to sit for this portrait.

Chapter Sixteen

Becoming A Target Of The Vice Squad

To be clear, Barry was never part of the criminal fraternity when he ran the Cine & Arts Club, and he assured me he didn't ever do anything against the law. "Quite the opposite, in fact," he once said in a strangely cryptic tone. But it was impossible in the 'Swinging Sixties' to have a club in Soho and not be on the fringes of the world of 'celebrity villains'.

The club was on an upper floor at 18 Greek Street. Peter Cook and Dudley Moore's The Establishment Club was now a 'blue' cinema showing pornographic films – which were largely illegal in those days. Soho in the 1970s and 1980s was well-known for the sex trade, but at the end of the 1960s, this was only just starting to become established. The cinema downstairs attracted a lot of villains, like flies round a honey pot. And they naturally drifted upstairs to Barry's club, where they could get a drink, some simple food like steak and chips, and a dark corner to plan out their next job.

I would sit at the bar and chat with the barmaid, Frankie, a sharp-faced woman with short dark hair and a mouth that turned down at the corners as if she was constantly disappointed in everything around her. Perhaps that was because she knew exactly what was going on in the club.

"That table over there," she said one evening, as she polished a glass. "That's Ronnie Knight with his brothers. He's been involved in a few criminal jobs, but nothing major." She checked the glass against the light and picked up another, using it to gesture at the beehived blonde sitting with Ronnie Knight, who seemed to hang on his every word. "That's his wife, the actress Barbara Windsor. Did you catch any of the *Carry On* films?" I shook my head. "Yeah, well, she's in a few of those."

"I'm not really a fan of the *Carry On*s," I said.

She nodded, as if that was the subject closed. "Now that table over there. That man with his bird, that's Eddie Chapman." Frankie said the name like I should have known it, but it wasn't one I recognised. The man, who looked in his fifties, was in a sharp double-breasted suit and had swept-back oiled hair. The girl – who was perhaps half his age – was a pretty brunette, her bouffant hair held back by a wide pink headband. I shook my head.

"You haven't heard of Eddie Chapman?" Frankie asked. "He was a small-time crook before the war and got recruited as a spy. But he played one side off against the other, so that both our lot and the Germans became convinced that he was working for each of them against the other." She picked up a new glass and started drying it. "To this day, no-one's quite sure exactly who he *was* working for."

At that moment Chapman patted the girl's hand and came up to the bar. "A Double Diamond for me and a rum and Coke for the bird, if you would, Frankie, love," he said. As the barmaid prepared the drinks, Chapman turned to me. His face was as sharp as his suit; the pencil moustache putting me in mind of a less-appealing version of Errol Flynn. "Hello gorgeous," he drawled. "You on your own?" Seemingly without shame, given that his girlfriend – or date? – was watching, he moved a little closer. "What's a smart piece like you doing on your own here?"

I shrugged. "Supporting my husband. It's his club."

He had the grace to look a little embarrassed. "Oh, ah. I see." As if to cover this, he pulled out a roll of banknotes and paid Frankie. Without looking back he took the drinks to his table. The girl gave him a frown as he sat.

"Nicely handled, Mrs Gregory," Frankie observed to me.

The girl's frown got deeper, and now she seemed to be giving Chapman a piece of her mind.

He held up a hand and responded with something that looked like an attempt to pacify her.

This seemed to have the opposite effect. She threw her drink in his face.

Shooting a brief look at me, she got up and tottered purposefully on her heels over to the hat-check girl. Once she had her coat, she walked out with a dismissive sweep of her bouffant hairdo.

Frankie and I shared a look of amusement. "Seems like he got what was coming," Frankie said, as Chapman tried to dab the rum and Coke off his suit with a handkerchief.

"Can't have been much of a spy," I observed.

A few minutes later there was a braying laugh from the other side of the room. Frankie indicated two men and a dark-haired girl. "There's a table of the film folk," she pointed out. "That's Kenneth Williams, who just laughed."

I gave a small gasp as I recognised the man next to him. "Oh," I said. "Isn't that David Hemmings?" He was gorgeous looking with floppy blond hair. Although he had dark, brooding eyes, he was currently smiling, as if it was him who had just made the joke that caused Kenneth Williams to bray. The girl gave a laugh as well; a throaty chuckle that seemed to come from too much gin and cigarettes. "That's Fenella Fielding," Frankie observed. "She's also been in a *Carry On*."

A fleshy, balding man came to the bar. While Frankie served him I 'carried on' taking in the people and décor of the club. From the low lighting, booth tables and red velvet curtains to the dog-eared movie posters on the walls, everything about the club was just a little tired, a little faded. I made a mental note to tell Barry the place needed sprucing up.

"That was Jess Yates," Frankie said, as the fleshy man walked away with his drinks. She tapped her pointed nose and gave me a small wink. "I can tell you things about that man," she said quietly, "but I wouldn't rat on him."

I knew better than to ask her to give anything away. Frankie's discretion was legendary; you could confide your darkest secrets to her, knowing they would go no further. To me, she was a beautiful person – not in the aesthetic sense; she was all sharp angles and pointy bits – but because of her fierce loyalty to her friends. I tried to capture that later, when I did a collage portrait of her; I had her looking 'the other way', to show she was always the 'soul of discretion.'

Of course, this beauty was wasted on the judge when she was had up for burglary, and he sent her down for a stretch in Holloway. She might have been loyal to her friends, but she clearly didn't give a fig for the strangers she stole from.

The secret Frankie held about Jess Yates intrigued me, and many years later I think I found out what it might have been. This was when it was revealed that his daughter, Paula Yates (presenter, writer, and wife of Bob Geldof), was most probably fathered by Jess's bitter TV rival, Hughie Green.

∽∾

Being above a 'blue' cinema showing porno flicks had further implications for Barry; it even resulted in him getting a couple of visits from the police's Soho Vice Squad.

The first of these apparently resulted from his casual generosity. The Cine and Arts Club had a cupboard on the ground floor that was meant to be for the storage of post and stuff like that, but generally it was left empty. According to Barry, the cinema manager, Mr Watkins, asked if he could use it instead.

"I said he could," Barry told me one morning. "And I wish I'd said no."

"Why?" I asked, looking up from mopping up the baby food Wayne had just thrown across the table.

"Because the cheeky sod was using it to store the dodgiest porno films. The ones so dirty you aren't allowed to show them." He wiped up a ring of baby food I'd missed from where Wayne's bowl had been. "When the police turned up saying they were looking for the films, and asked to see in the cupboard, he told them it was mine. Presumably to throw them off the scent. But the police forced the lock and found the stash of illegal smut."

"Oh, Barry," I said. "Will you be prosecuted?"

He gave me his boyish smile. "I don't think so, Annabelle," he replied, putting his hand on my arm. "When they came up to the club and accused me, I pointed out that I have no means of showing any film – smutty or otherwise – and said I had let Watkins use the cupboard. I asked them which was more likely: a club owner – without a projector or a screen – keeping dirty films, or a blue cinema manager using an empty cupboard to store his dodgy films?" He laughed. "I said it was much more likely they belonged to Watkins."

"And they agreed?"

He hesitated for a long moment. "Yes," he said eventually. "I think we're now in full agreement." Then he added, "Although all the villains who'd been drinking in the club disappeared down the back stairs quick as a flash when the coppers were pounding up like a herd of elephants, shouting 'Police raid!'."

After that the Soho Vice Squad left the club alone for many months, and Barry assured me everything was OK on that front. Until one morning, when they switched their attention away from the club, and made their second raid. On our house in Goldhurst Terrace.

It happened very early in the morning. Barry and I were asleep, and thankfully neither Marcus, Wayne, nor baby Sacha had yet woken up.

I was vaguely aware of a knock on the front door, but must have decided I'd dreamt it, and turned over to sleep again. Then there was a nudge in my ribs, and Barry hissed, "Annabelle, Annabelle! Wake up! There's someone at the door!"

I squinted at the clock. "Nonsense," I muttered. "It's half five."

Then we both heard the knock again, and this time a voice shouted, "Police! Vice Squad! Open up!"

Barry leapt out of bed and threw on his dressing gown, exclaiming, "They'll wake the whole street!"

My concern was more what all our neighbours would think if they heard who was doing the raid. The *Vice Squad!* "Quick," I yelled. "Let them in!"

When I'd put on my housecoat and got downstairs, a solid-looking grey-haired detective in a crumpled suit was standing in the hall with three uniformed officers.

"Mister Barry Gregory?" the detective was asking.

"Yes," Barry replied, his voice slowed with cautious curiosity. "What is this about?"

The detective showed his warrant card. "Detective Sergeant Perkins. We have reason to believe there are pornographic materials on these premises in contravention to the Obscene Publications Act 1959." He held up a piece of paper, then whipped it back into his pocket before I could read it. "We have a warrant to search the premises."

"Come now, Detective Sergeant," Barry said, with an easy smile, "I think we both know this is quite unnecessary. I have made it clear we have nothing whatsoever to do with the cinema downstairs from the club."

"That is the *Cine*," Perkins emphasised the word, "and Arts Club?"

"It is," Barry said with a small sigh. "But it's called that because we have clientele from the world of film and from the arts. Not because we show any films: dirty or otherwise."

"Yes, I've heard about your clientele," Perkins muttered darkly. "Not all from the cinema and arts." He gave the nod to his men, and said, "But we'll just check on the filthy films, shall we?"

Barry gave a deeper sigh. "If you must. But as I say, this really is quite unnecessary. I'm sure..." He paused, in a way he often did if he wanted to give greater emphasis to his words. "...we can sort it out." When Perkins remained silent, he continued, "But please be careful. We have small children asleep upstairs."

Perkins nodded to his men. Two went upstairs, while the third pushed past us and went straight into the sitting room. Perkins stayed with us, shooting suspicious glances, as if he expected we would try something. We stood in silence, listening to the thumping of boots and the opening of doors as his constables went through the rooms. "You all right, love?" Barry asked me quietly.

"I feel sick," I replied. "Those men going through all our things."

"If there's nothing to find, you've got nothing to fear," Perkins observed.

Barry faced him, arms crossed. "You and I both know there's nothing here, Detective Sergeant." He paused again. "So if they *do* find anything, it won't have been put there by me. If you get my meaning?" Perkins said nothing, but I sensed the standoff between the two men, like a pair of lions facing each other across an African plain. "You work for Detective Chief Superintendent Bill Moody, I assume?" Barry asked, a sneer in his voice.

"Yes."

"Well, please let Mister Moody know what I just said, would you?"

Perkins's men came back, and he gave them the smallest shake of his head, as if to tell them not to say what they might have been planning. He shepherded them out the door, then stopped on the threshold. "I'll tell him, Mister Gregory," he said, "but Mister Moody is quite the stickler. He likes things to be all neat and tidy." Barry said nothing, so Perkins continued, "He likes to know that debts will always be paid. He wouldn't want you, your lovely wife, and your three children to be woken up by this sort of thing on a regular basis, if you get *my* meaning."

A couple of months later Barry closed the club, saying the outgoings were too high, and it was no longer giving a realistic income. After that he never ran any sort of establishment in Soho again.

According to my internet search, in 1977 Detective Chief Superintendent Bill Moody was tried for corruption. He was apparently found guilty and sentenced to twelve years in prison. It seems that the corruption was widespread throughout Soho, with entertainment establishments paying 'protection' money to the police. Not paying might then leave them open to being raided.

'The Bistro Window'

Collage. 30cm x 25cm.

This bust was a feature in the Bistro window. I originally bought it at an antique market. I forget where – but I do remember how antique markets became such a big part of our lives.

Chapter Seventeen

Becoming Madeline From M&S

Our daughter Sacha was born in 1968. Since the births of Marcus in 1963 and Wayne the year after, I had been steadily rebuilding my modelling career – so that by the time my third baby bump was showing, I once again had a strong portfolio of TV ads and still photo-shoots under my ever-expanding belt.

Such was the ongoing demand for my services, that when I told the directors, photographers and agents I would need to take a few months off either side of the birth, they simply worked around my dates, scheduling assignments for when I planned to be back. When Barry stopped working at the Cine & Arts Club, my income alone was enough to keep the family finances looking pretty healthy.

But it soon became clear that Barry was uncomfortable with me being the sole breadwinner.

"I need to be doing something," he complained over a drink in an atmospheric 'olde worlde' pub one evening. "It's not right for a man to be living off his wife's earnings."

"You could find another restaurant or club," I suggested. "Stick to what you know."

He shook his head. "No. I want to try something different. Something where I'm not beholden to anyone else. Where I'm fully in charge of my own fortunes." He tapped his fingers on the table, gazing around at the old paintings and brassware that decorated the pub. Suddenly he looked back at me, his eyes shining. "Antiques," he said. "That's it. I'll buy and sell antiques." He tapped his fingers again. "You remember that chap we used to meet in the Partisan, Wolf Mankowitz?"

I nodded. Wolf had been one of the investors in the café. He'd not only been a film scriptwriter, but also a successful antiques dealer.

Barry continued, "He made it seem an easy trade to get into. So long as you buy stuff that's undervalued – from house clearances or from small traders who don't know what they've got – you can clean it up and sell it on for a profit." His eyes shone even more. "You can make a fortune if you know what you're doing."

I didn't want to be the one to point out the obvious flaw in his plan while he was so excited, but one of us had to be practical. "You don't know what you're doing, Barry," I stated. "And you'll need somewhere to keep all the stock, somewhere to work on it, as well as somewhere to sell it." The subject of money also came to mind. "And you'll need to fund your initial stock. That'll take some cash."

He shrugged. "I've got a bit put by from the sale of the club. And we can use the garage at the house to keep and work on the stock. And there's a market in Hampstead on Sundays. I can sell it there. Marcus can come along, too." He gave me his boyish smile. "Come on, Annabelle love, what's life if you don't take a risk or two? I can learn the trade, just like I learned all about hospitality. It can't be that difficult; there'll be plenty of books I can read, or courses I can go on."

"And you'll really want to let go of hospitality?" I asked. It had been his whole life almost as long as I had known him.

"Of course," he assured me, the fires of enthusiasm seeming to burn strong. "From now on, it's antiques all the way."

Except, of course, it wasn't. It was also cooking and selling sausages at the antiques market. "The smell is a perfect way to draw in the punters," he told me. And it was restoring old paintings. "Nobody wants a dirty painting. They want one they can see and appreciate".

And then it was buying and selling motor cars. "The more expensive the car, the bigger the profit margins" – a venture that resulted in me driving the kids to school in a Rolls-Royce (which I found embarrassing), and wrapping a hot-rod painted hearse – yes, you read that correctly – around a post-box. But I'll tell those stories in a later chapter.

※

To give Barry his due, the antiques business did work out for him, and it was also something Marcus and I became involved in, especially as, when I turned thirty, the modelling assignments from Jilly Norton (who was acting as my agent), were starting to thin out a little. Not suddenly on the day of my birthday, but gradually I began to realise I wasn't getting so much work. The good news was this freed me up to become more involved in the antiques.

When it came to art restoration, Barry decided he needed to know what he was doing, so he went on a one-week course in the Welsh mountains with his friend John. The course covered things like repairing ripped paintings, which Barry did find useful a few times in his antiques career, as well as general cleaning and restoration.

John told me later that Barry was a model student on the course and applied himself diligently to learning his trade. I was constantly impressed by his increasing skill and knowledge when it came to antique art.

While they might have studied hard during the day, it seemed they partied pretty hard in the evenings. Perhaps Barry wanted to show the Welsh that Englishmen could drink too. It seems he and John found a couple of excellent Welsh pubs, and when they had drunk the first one dry of whisky, they'd moved on to the second. I have no doubt they would have cleaned that one out as well, if they'd had the time.

Barry certainly looked quite flushed when he got home at the end of the week.

As a family, we all had our roles to play in the antiques business; Barry was the buyer and chief seller of the antiques, as well as the genial sausage chef. Marcus was his 'mini-me' assistant, carrying small packages, cleaning pieces for sale, and generally being a 'cute kid' to pull the punters to the pitch at the open-air market in Hampstead.

I, on the other hand, became both buyer and seller in the 'fashion and fabric wing' of our antique business. I had pointed out to Barry that fashion and textiles were something I knew a fair bit about, and that my contacts in that world – the wardrobe people, seamstresses and costumiers – could be an invaluable source of both information and actual clothing.

In weeks when I had time around any shoots, my mornings were spent hunting down sellable stock. As soon as I had the kids up and fed, the boys off to school and Sacha in the care of her child-minder, I was out of the door with my shoulder bag full of more bags – as you never knew how many you'd need.

I would have already scoured the obituary columns of the local papers, looking particularly for old ladies with an upmarket address. I'd get on to the house-clearance firms and see if they had already cleared out all the deceased's stuff. Then I'd be straight round to see what they'd got. Often, I'd strike it lucky, picking up something from the 20s or 30s, such as a low-waisted flapper number, a carefully preserved wedding dress that would appeal to the modern woman in love with retro, or maybe some lace tablecloths. I was also on the look-out for any costume jewellery, particularly strings of pearls and zirconium brooches or rings. Bangles were a big thing in those days, so I was particularly keen to find any I could bundle up and sell as a job lot.

I built up a network of removal men too, and would pop my head round their doors to see if they had a downsizing coming up. They would tip me off about the kind of family and the stuff they might be throwing out.

On Fridays, I'd go to the Portobello Road Market and work my way through the stalls, looking for things like Edwardian lace, 1930s satin evening gowns, World War 2 utility wear or beaded 1920s shawls.

If I had a photo shoot, I would be asking the wardrobe mistress if she or any of her seamstresses had anything they didn't want, and I managed to pick up some good pieces this way as well.

In the afternoons I would bear my prizes back to the house, where I would repair, clean and sort the garments. I would mend any torn seams, restore any missing buttons or ribbons, then steam-press everything ready for sale.

On market Sundays, Barry, Marcus and I would leave the house no later than 5:30 a.m., having packed our old Bedford van the night before with all my stock, Barry's antique furniture and decorative pieces, together with plenty of packs of sausages to go on the barbecue. I would also have a folding table with a lace cloth, a clothes rail, and some jewellery boxes to display the pieces I had bought. The van was an impressive find; Barry had bought it off a rock band (he never did tell me which one), for the princely sum of £16. The back was covered in a thick shag-pile carpet, which Barry told me had been to protect the drums and instruments that the band were carting around. I remember looking him squarely in the eye when he told me this.

"Seriously, Barry? Thick carpet in the back of a van used by a rock band – and you say it was to protect the instruments?

Not for something else perhaps? Something with the groupies?"

He gave me back a look of studied innocence.

"That's what they told me, Annabelle. And I have no reason to doubt them."

Needless to say, I gave the carpet a thorough clean before I put anything of ours onto it.

Often, we'd see our neighbour while we were packing the van. Tony was a slim man in his forties, with a slightly camp manner – for all he was married to a lovely Viennese woman called Helga – and we would often dine at each other's houses. He would drift up and observe us as we carried our things from the garage and loaded them into the van.

"I'm never afraid of hard work," he'd often say, as Barry or I struggled with something heavy or bulky. "I can watch it for hours."

We'd smile politely at the joke and carry on loading.

By six the next morning we'd be setting up our pitch in the field close to the Hampstead Theatre. Barry would soon have the barbecue going, and he'd be serving sausages in buns to me, Marcus and the other stallholders. When the public were let in at nine, he'd become the genial trader, switching effortlessly between the chef serving succulent sausages one moment, and the knowledgeable dealer spinning all sorts of stories around the antiques the next (some of which were even true).

Meanwhile I'd be keeping an eye on the women flicking through my clothing rails or textile boxes, looking for any expressions of interest. If a potential buyer took an item of clothing and held it up before the mirror, I would casually drift up and say something like, "What style are you looking for?" then get into a conversation around the piece. It generally seemed to work. I got a real buzz from making a sale, and seeing a happy customer walk away with an antique dress, skirt or tablecloth, or a piece of costume jewellery she would enjoy wearing.

Being a successful model, I did sometimes get recognised. It would start with a curious look or maybe a frown, then the question, "Aren't you that girl off the telly?" Or perhaps they would vaguely recognise me and jump to the conclusion that they must have met me socially. I'd get things like, "Don't I know you from somewhere?" I tended to keep quiet, to see where this would go. After a moment, there would be a clicking of fingers and something like, "I know! You're Janice's friend, aren't you? We met at her dinner party the other week!" Before I could respond, there'd be some more finger clicking, then, "Don't tell me, don't tell me..." and the moment of triumphant recall. "Madeline! It's Madeline, isn't it! You work at M&S!"

Always aware of the amused smile from Barry earwigging behind me, I'd decide whether I would let it go, or put them right. Sometimes I would just smile, nod and enquire politely if they were interested in anything – from a sausage up to a 1920s wedding dress. Or I might say, "No that's not me, but you might have seen some of my modelling work." Given that my face looked out from almost every shop counter as I clutched a Barclaycard, and there were countless of my ads on TV, it always amused me that they didn't know where they'd seen me.

"It's because they're meeting you out of context," Barry suggested one evening, as we sat round the kitchen table writing up our sales for the day in the ledger. "They could have seen you on the TV last night, but if they then see you at a market stall the next morning, there's nothing to make the connection." He gave me a pat on the hand. "And anyway love, I can see it amuses you to string them along."

"It opens the conversation," I replied.

"And puts them on the back foot," he added. "You are good at turning it round and making a sale, whether it's for your stuff or mine." He tapped the numbers in the ledger. "We made a fair bit today. A hundred and forty-eight pounds and fifty pence."

"We make a great team," I said with a smile.

"That's true," he said.

Which made his behaviour a few months later all the more awful.

'People on a Beach in Cumbria'

Pencil on paper. 42cm x 30cm.

This sketch was done on a holiday in the seaside village of St. Bees, Cumbria.

Chapter Eighteen

Becoming Relaxed – The Calm Before The Storm

It was early summer. The schools were about to break up, and I decided we needed a family holiday. Sacha had a friend in her infant school called Becky, whose mother, Joanna, had a place up in St Bees. This was a coastal town on the edge of the Irish Sea in Cumbria; a picturesque location full of pebble beaches, mudflats and sweeping cliffs.

Joanna and I had got talking outside the school one afternoon.

"This daily grind is getting me down," I observed, as we waited for the kids to come out. "And when school breaks up, they'll be under my feet all day." I'd been a bit light on modelling at that point and was spending much of my time at home with the three children.

"It's relentless, being a mum, isn't it?" she replied.

I gave a hollow laugh. "I vowed when my eldest was a baby that he'd be brought up in a warm, loving household," I said.

"And is he?" she asked, one eyebrow arched.

"Yeah..." I paused. "But it's one thing committing to it when you've got a single child, and quite another when you've got a ten-year-old, a nine-year-old and a five-year-old running around fighting and screaming all day long."

Joanna nodded. "You need to get away," she said in a pragmatic tone. "Jack and I have a holiday cottage near the sea up north, and we go up there whenever we can. You, Barry and the kids should take a place in the same town for the summer. The children can run wild, and you can relax." She smiled. "Barbecues on the beach and wine in the evenings. What's not to like?"

"It sounds idyllic," I said, as Sacha and Becky emerged together and ran across the playground to the gates, then bundled into each of our arms. "Are you serious?" I added, as Sacha clasped me around the waist. "You really mean it?"

"Of course." She stopped to look at a coloured crayon picture being held up by Becky. "Lovely, darling... What is it?"

"Silly Mummy! It's a pony!"

Joanna nodded, squinting at the picture. "Right... It's very good." She looked up. "We usually suggest people stay in the Queen's Hotel. It's really just a pub, but it's very comfortable. I can get you a couple of rooms if you like?"

When I got home, I told Barry. "It's perfect," I said. "The kids can all play by the water's edge, and the two boys can get into sailing. You and I can walk on the cliffs and the beaches. I've really missed being in the middle of nature." I looked up at him. "It's why my art has suffered, you know. We're spending all our time in the middle of London, and it's getting me down. I need to feel part of the countryside again." Warming to my theme, I tried to make him understand my need to get out of the city; to feel at one with nature – and for a moment it was as if I was once again little Annabelle playing in the trees at Whyteleafe. "I want to paint views across the hills and the lakes," I said. "And explore all the colours and shapes of the plants."

"Of course," Barry said. "Sounds lovely." Something in his tone made me frown. It was said in a way that seemed to have a big *but*... hanging off it. "But..." he continued, "I've got too much on here to go away right now. There's a house on Campden Hill Road that's being cleared, and I've put in offers on several pieces. There's a breakfront tallboy, a couple of Regency mahogany tables and a stunning chair with cabriole legs. Plus a painting attributed to Allan Ramsay. If my offer's accepted, and I am pretty certain it will be, they'll all need checking and perhaps some restoration work if I'm going to get them into an auction coming up in Chiswick. It's a special sale and I don't want to miss it."

His over-long explanation didn't move me. "That's as maybe, Barry," I said. "But..." and here I gave my own emphasis to the word, "...you need time off. Time with your family. There'll be other tallboys. Other paintings, whether attributed to Allan Ramsay or whoever else. You need to relax."

He shook his head. "I can't let this one pass, Annabelle." He paused, his eyes flicking across mine. "You go. Have a good time with the kids. I'll stay here. If I get this deal done right, it could be worth many hundreds of pounds. Even a thousand or more. And I've got several other deals bubbling under as well. You go."

I could see it was not worth arguing and gave in. My only stipulation was that he shouldn't work too hard, and I said I would write when we got there.

I called Joanna and explained it would just be me and the kids, and she said that was fine.

"How long are you planning on staying?" she asked.

I gave this some thought. "If Barry's not coming, we can stay longer."

"We'll be there for the whole summer holiday," she said. "Why don't you do the same?"

"The full six weeks?" That seemed a long time – but the more I thought about it, the better it seemed. Enough time for a really good summer break. Enough time to relax in the countryside and on the beach; enough time to enjoy being with the kids.

I drove up to St Bees in the Alfa Romeo Berlina we'd originally bought when we'd moved to Goldhurst Terrace. I put Marcus in the front with me, while Wayne and Sacha fought in the back seat. In those days there were no rules about seat belts or child restraints, so the kids were free to bounce around inside the car like they were at an adventure playground. After a while I gave up shouting at them to sit still, while games of I Spy, or 'spot the white car' were quickly forgotten.

The journey was mainly on the motorways and only took around six hours; the M1 and the M6 were virtually empty in those days. It would have been quicker, if it were not for the frequent stops for food and drink, then the consequent stops for a pee. These were uncoordinated; each child deciding they needed a pee individually, so we had to stop three times more often than would have been necessary, had they all managed to go at the same time.

Thus it was a somewhat frazzled Annabelle who finally parked outside the pub, a pretty little building with ivy-covered walls in Main Street, St Bees. Thankfully the kids had finally gone to sleep somewhere after Carnforth; Sacha and Wayne cuddled together on the back seat, while Marcus was stretched out beneath them in the footwell.

As I was trying to decide how best to get them out of the car without waking them, Joanna came up.

"Annabelle!" she called out; a big grin on her face.

"Joanna!" We gave each other a hug.

"How was the journey?"

I muttered something about having to stop frequently.

"Kids! They're all the same. Becky is just as bad."

I realised Joanna was alone. "Where is she?" I asked.

"In bed right now, but she's really looking forward to seeing Sacha tomorrow." She glanced towards the car. "Your lot are very quiet just now."

"They're all asleep," I said. "Can you give me a hand getting them into their room without waking them up?"

She helped me ease each child out of the car and carry them up to a room with three beds. Once the kids were safely under the covers, we went down to the bar and ordered a couple of large glasses of wine.

"Have you made any plans?" Joanna asked. "You've got six weeks to enjoy up here."

Six weeks! Six whole weeks! Away from the smoke and grime of London!

I relaxed into my chair and took a sip of wine. "I just want to let the kids run around and do whatever they want. They can exhaust themselves during the day and sleep well at night."

"And you?"

"I want to explore the beauty of the seaside and the cliffs, and to paint as much of it as possible."

Later, in my room, I dug around in my luggage and found my writing pad, a pen and a set of envelopes. *Dear Barry*, I wrote. *We've arrived OK, and the kids are asleep in their room. Joanna is so welcoming, and I'm sure we'll have a great time.* I paused, tapping the top of the pen against my teeth. What else to tell him? *I'm so looking forward to getting out and doing some painting. It's been too long since I did anything. I might even see if there are any life classes in Whitehaven or one of the other towns nearby. There must be a thriving artist community in such a picturesque place.* I thought a bit more, then added, *I miss you, Barry. Do you know, we've hardly had more than a day apart since we got married? I'm already looking forward to being with you again in six weeks, and I'm sure the kids are too. But in the meantime, we're going to have a lovely holiday here. I'll write every day, so you know how we're doing. Write back and let me know how things are with you. Did the Campden Hill Road house clearance go OK? Let me know. Lots of love, Annabelle x.*

Barry must have been very busy, because he didn't seem to find the time to write back. But over the six weeks, I put that out of my mind, throwing myself into the holiday activities with Joanna and the children. The boys tried sailing on the sea in little gaff-rigged boats called scows, while Sacha and Becky played on the beach. Joanna and I sat on towels and watched.

Ten-year-old Marcus took well to sailing, soon becoming very proficient at steering the little craft around the buoys and even winning some races organised by the local sailing club. Wayne, at nine, was less sure and needed a lot more encouragement by his mother shouting from the shore. Sacha, at five, was content to splash in the shallows and run up and down the bank collecting pebbles. This was until Joanna took us to a riding school catering for smaller children. Sacha was put onto a short, barrel-shaped pony. Sitting there, with her little legs splayed out almost at right angles, she broke into a big grin and said, "This is such fun, Mummy!" The teacher led the pony into a walk and Sacha clutched the reins and settled into the saddle like a natural. I couldn't help thinking that she was taking to it almost as if this was her tenth lesson, not her first. "Can I do this every day, Mummy?" she asked.

"Of course, Sacha darling," I answered. For the rest of the holiday, I dropped her off four mornings a week, picking her up at lunchtime. On the way home each day, I was regaled by her childish chatter. "The pony's called Shamrock, Mummy," she told me one time. "I tell him he's a good boy, and I stroke his neck, and I give him food, and he eats it out of my hand, but I have to keep my hand flat or he might bite my fingers."

She made a short pause for breath, and I managed to get in, "Do be careful, darling."

"I am careful, Mummy, I am, and Shamrock wouldn't bite me anyway, 'cos he loves me, and I love him, and Miss Fishlock says if I'm a good girl, they'll let me brush him down after riding, but that means I have to stay an extra hour after riding, and that's another fifty pence each day, so is it OK, Mummy? Can I stay? Please say 'yes', Mummy, please!"

Of course I did let her stay, and the extra 50p was a small price to pay to see her little face glowing with pleasure. Even if it was me paying the stable for the privilege of my child doing their job for them.

Wayne took to finding stretches of mudbank, where he would spend hours poking and prodding the mud with a stick, before using it to dig out any objects he found. Not only did he get filthy every day, so that I was continually having to take his clothes to the laundrette, but I was also presented with his stinking finds to admire. From mud-filled bottles to a rusted padlock and even an old Timex watch, these all had to be meticulously cleaned so he could put them carefully in the wooden box we bought in the local hardware shop.

And all the time I was with the kids, I was painting, carrying my easel, pad and paints wherever I went. Joanna would very kindly keep an eye on whichever of the children wasn't in some formally supervised activity, while I concentrated on my painting, enjoying the inner peace I have always felt while trying to capture the stunning beauty of the world as a picture on the paper.

It was a considerably less frazzled and much more relaxed Annabelle who gave Joanna a big farewell hug, then packed the kids and the luggage into the Alfa Romeo. Even the six-hour journey back to Goldhurst Terrace didn't stress me out (too much). I'd had a lovely holiday with my children, I was back into painting, and I was coming home to the man I loved.

But I was not prepared – not even in the slightest – for what I found when we got back.

When we got home, I was so excited to see Barry again, that I told the kids to leave the luggage in the car and led them straight up to the front door. I opened it and went in to the hall with a call of "Barry? Barry love? We're home!"

But there was no answering shout, no delighted husband running down the stairs and clasping me in his arms, no father welcoming his children home after six weeks away.

Marcus, Wayne and Sacha came in behind me. "Where's Daddy?" Wayne asked.

"I don't know," I replied, putting on a smile. "Maybe he's gone out. I'm sure he'll be home soon."

Marcus went into the kitchen. "Urgh!" he exclaimed. "It smells in here."

I followed him in and was immediately hit with a smell of rancid cooking fat. Putting my hand over my nose, I went over to what seemed to be the source – the open oven door. I could see immediately where the smell was coming from; there was hardened fat all over the inside, with a semi-liquid pool at the bottom.

"Why hasn't Daddy cleaned it?" Sacha asked.

"I don't know," I replied. "But I'm sure he'll have a reason when he gets home." Frankly, I couldn't imagine what that would be; I'd left the house in pristine condition and wasn't expecting Barry to let it get so dirty.

His reason had better be good.

We went into the sitting room. Again, this was very scruffy, while I had left it beautifully tidy. There were ring stains on the coffee table, cushions thrown onto the floor instead of neatly placed along the back of the sofa, and... my eyes flicked back to the coffee table.

Why were there two wine glasses standing there?

Sensing Marcus behind me, I quickly gathered the glasses up, concerned he might jump to the same conclusion I had: that his father had been entertaining someone while we were away. I glanced at one of the glasses...

Someone wearing lipstick...

I took the glasses back to the kitchen and put them by the sink, carefully turning the pink smear to the back and hopefully away from curious eyes. "Come on kids," I said brightly, "let's go unpack the car."

I led them outside and handed each one their bag from the car boot. "Take those in, and up to your rooms." As Sacha clutched her bag and followed her brothers up the path as fast as her little legs could go, I heard a footstep behind me.

I spun round. It was our neighbour, Tony.

"Annabelle..." he began, and I could see from his white face that he was in some kind of distress. "Oh, Annabelle." He drew me into his arms and gave me a tight hug.

"What is it, Tony?" I mumbled into his cashmere shoulder.

He let me go and held me at arm's length, upset written all over his thin face. "Annabelle, I..." He took a deep breath. "I'm so sorry."

"What is it, Tony?" I insisted. "Tell me." I already knew from the lipstick what he was most likely going to reveal. But I needed to hear it said.

Sure enough it was as bad as I feared.

"Barry's had a woman coming and going all the time you've been away," he said, his eyes as wide as saucers.

I stared at him in horror. So it was true; Barry really *had* been unfaithful!

No wonder he hadn't wanted to come to Cumbria.

No wonder he hadn't replied to any of my letters.

No wonder he hadn't taken the time to clean the house, even though he would have known we were coming home today.

He'd been 'otherwise engaged'.

Marcus, Wayne and Sacha Gregory

My three beautiful children – Wayne (top), Marcus (middle) and Sacha (bottom).

Chapter Nineteen

Becoming Stronger

I managed to get the kids to bed, and stood in the living room, contemplating the mess. It looked scruffy, uncared for. The more I looked, the more I spotted; dirty plates on the floor beside Barry's chair, newspapers scattered across the carpet, an overflowing ashtray. Six weeks of bachelor living laid bare.

If only it had been bachelor living.

There was the sound of the front door opening, then closing and being locked. Footsteps going into the kitchen.

Without moving or making a sound, I waited.

The kettle gave a steamy scream from the stove.

Water was poured into a mug.

I picked up a cushion from the floor and thumped it onto the sofa with more force than necessary. The wine glasses were by the kitchen sink, but I could still see that lipstick mark in my mind's eye. Coral pink. Not my shade.

Barry appeared in the doorway, coffee mug in hand, looking annoyingly refreshed for someone who should be mired in guilt. He surveyed the chaos with what seemed like mild surprise, as if seeing it properly for the first time.

"Place got a bit untidy," he observed, taking a sip.

I bent to collect a plate smeared with what looked like the remnants of cheese on toast. "A bit untidy?" I straightened up and faced him. "Barry, there was a wine glass with lipstick."

He didn't flinch. Didn't even have the decency to look embarrassed. "Yes," he said simply.

The plate trembled in my hands. I'd been rehearsing this moment for the last twenty minutes, imagining denials, excuses, pleading. But this flat acknowledgment was somehow worse. It felt like indifference.

"Is that all you're going to say? Yes?"

"What would you like me to say, Annabelle?" He put his mug down on the coffee table, next to one of the ring stains. "Would you prefer I lied to you?"

"I'd prefer you hadn't done it in the first place." My voice was rising despite my efforts to stay calm. The children were upstairs; I didn't want them to hear this. "Who is she?"

"Does it matter?"

"Of course it bloody matters!" The plate clattered as I set it down harder than intended. "I'm your wife. I spent six weeks writing to you every day, telling you how much I missed you, how much the children missed you. And here you were with... with..."

"Anneliese. Her name's Anneliese."

The name hit me like I'd been punched in the belly. It made her real. Not just a lipstick mark, but a person with a name, someone who'd sat in my living room, drunk from my glasses, maybe even slept in my bed. The thought made my stomach lurch.

"Anneliese?"

"She's Dutch."

The image of a hard-faced woman in traditional Dutch dress with the wooden clogs and lace bonnet came to mind. Not a beauty. 'Cloggy' – that's what this woman would always be in my mind.

"And how long has this been going on?"

Barry moved to the window and stood with his back to me, his hands buried in his pockets. "A few months," he muttered into the curtain.

A few months! While I'd been working with him at the antique markets. While I'd been getting the children ready for school. Taking them to Cubs and football. Putting them to bed. While I'd looked after them on what should have been the family holiday. The one he'd had no intention of taking.

"Turn around when I'm talking to you."

He did, slowly, and I saw something in his face that might have been shame. Or more likely just irritation at being confronted.

"Do you love her?" The question escaped before I could stop it, and I immediately wished I could take it back. I didn't want to hear the answer.

"I don't know." He shrugged, and that casual gesture made me want to throw something at him. "It's not about love, Annabelle. It's about..."

"It's about what? About you being bored? About me not being enough?"

"It's not about you."

"Of course it's about me!" I grabbed another cushion and hurled it onto the sofa. "I'm your wife! When you sleep with someone else, it's absolutely about me!"

Barry rubbed his forehead like he was developing a headache. "Look, I know you're upset..."

"Upset?" I gave a bitter, humourless laugh. "Barry, I feel like you've taken everything I thought I knew about us and thrown it in the bin. Six weeks I was away. Six weeks of thinking about you, missing you, writing to you every single day. And you couldn't even be bothered to reply."

"I was busy."

"Busy with her. With... Anneliese." He flinched at that. Good.

I sank onto the sofa, suddenly exhausted. The adrenaline that had carried me through the discovery, through getting the children settled, through this confrontation, was starting to ebb. In its place came something worse – a hollow ache that seemed to settle in my chest.

"I feel so stupid," I said quietly. "All those letters I wrote. All those times I told you I loved you, that I couldn't wait to see you again. You must have been laughing at me."

"I wasn't laughing at you, Annabelle."

"Then what? What was I to you while you were with her? Just the inconvenient wife you had to come home to?"

Barry sat on the other end of the sofa, carefully, as if I might throw something at him. "It wasn't like that."

"Then please tell me what it was like. Because I'm trying to understand how the man I've been married to for twelve years, the father of my children, could do this to us."

He was quiet for a long moment, staring at his hands. When he finally spoke, his voice was softer. "I felt trapped, Annabelle. Between the business and the house and the children... I felt like I was disappearing."

"So you found yourself with Clo... with Anneliese."

"Something like that."

I thought about my own father then, about the day he'd packed his suitcase and walked out for the final time. "Are you going to leave us?" I asked.

Barry looked up sharply. "Do you want me to?"

"I don't know what I want right now." I straightened one of the cushions. "But I know what I don't want." I took a shaky breath. "I don't want Marcus, Wayne and Sacha to grow up thinking their father abandoned them. I don't want them to have to explain to their friends why their father doesn't live with them anymore."

"Annabelle..."

"And I don't want to give up my house, my life, everything I've built, because you decided to have a ruddy affair." My voice was getting stronger now, fuelled by anger. An anger that felt cleansing. "And I don't want to give that woman the satisfaction of breaking up my family."

Barry shifted uncomfortably. "It's not about Anneliese getting satisfaction..."

"Isn't it? Don't tell me she doesn't know you're married. Don't tell me she hasn't been wondering when you're going to leave your wife for her."

He didn't answer, which was answer enough.

I stood up and began collecting the scattered newspapers, needing something to do with my hands. "So here's what's going to happen, Barry Gregory. You're going to end it with her. Today. Not tomorrow, not next week. Today."

"Annabelle, you can't just..."

"I can, and I will." I turned to face him, holding the newspapers against my chest like armour. "You want to be honest? Then let's be completely honest. You've broken something here, Barry. You've broken the trust that's taken, what is it... fourteen years since we first met? It's taken fourteen years to build, and I don't know if it can be fixed. But I'm willing to try, for the children's sake if nothing else."

"And for your sake?"

I considered this. What was left for my sake? The marriage I'd thought I had was gone. The man I'd married had turned out to be someone who could betray me while I was writing him letters. But there was still the house; the life we'd built. Still the children who needed stability.

"I don't know yet," I said honestly. "Right now, I feel like I don't know you at all. But I know I don't want to be another woman whose husband walked out on her. I won't be my mother."

Barry stood up too, and for a moment we faced each other across the coffee table, across the wreckage of what we'd been.

"So we stay together," he said slowly.

"We try to stay together. But it won't be the same, Barry. I can't just pretend this didn't happen. I can't just go back to believing that when you say you're off on a buying trip, or going to an auction, that's what you're actually doing."

"I understand."

"Do you? Because it means no more Anneliese. Dutch or any other nationality. It means no more affairs, no more lies. It means you're going to have to earn back my trust, and that's going to take time. Maybe forever."

He nodded, but I could see him weighing it up, calculating whether the price was worth paying. The fact that he had to think about it at all told me everything I needed to know about where we stood.

But he came to a good decision.

"I'll end it with Anneliese," he said finally.

"Phone her. Tonight."

"Tonight?"

"Tonight."

I turned back to tidying the room, stacking the papers, straightening the furniture. Making order from chaos, at least on the surface. "The children are going to sense something's wrong. Marcus found the smelly oven and saw the wine glasses. He's not stupid."

"What do we tell them?"

"Nothing, for now. We act normal. We give them stability while we figure out if we can make this work."

"And us? What do we do about us?"

I paused in my cleaning and looked at him. Really looked at him. He was still handsome, still the man I'd fallen in love with in a heartbeat at that Regent Street Poly hop all those years ago. But something had shifted. Lost its beauty. Reset.

"I don't know," I said. "I suppose we'll just have to find out."

'Life Drawing'

Charcoal on paper. 42cm x 60cm.

Getting back to life drawing was a key part of my 'reset' after Barry's affair. Joining life classes at the Camden School of Art was a form of therapy, and this picture was typical of the work I was doing at the time.

Chapter Twenty

Becoming an Artist Again

We stayed together.

For the next forty-one years, to be exact, until Barry died in 2014.

But one thing was for sure: life with Barry could never be the same again. This was partly because I found it hard to trust him; as I had said that evening, I could never be a hundred per cent sure that when he went out, he wasn't seeing cloggy old Anneliese again. Or maybe even some other new woman. But mostly because I decided I was not going to build my life around his convenience any more. I was going to make the most of myself. Have more 'me time', as I believe the young people call it nowadays.

If Barry could have his fun, then so could I. But not with another man, I wasn't thinking of that. Instead it was about doing more of what I wanted to do. And mostly that meant art.

After rediscovering my passion for painting and drawing in Cumbria (although I had destroyed almost all the paintings from the holiday after finding out about Barry's affair with Cloggy – somehow I couldn't bear to look at pictures I'd been doing so happily, whilst he'd been doing... her), I decided my art was going to become a much more structured part of my life. Never again would I let my painting and drawing suffer, now it was going to be second only to the kids. Non-negotiable.

"I'm going to do a life class one afternoon a week," I told him a few days later. "You'll have to look after the children."

He looked unsure. "Which afternoon?"

I pressed my advantage. "Wednesday at 4 p.m. I've been to the Camden School of Art, and they have a class. I'm going to enrol."

"Maybe you could pick the kids up before you go to Camden?"

"Oh no, Barry," I answered, putting my hands on my hips and giving him a hard stare. "I'm not going to be rushing and panicking before a class. I need to be relaxed and unstressed so I can draw or paint. You can pick them up from school and give them tea. Who knows," I added brightly, "you could even read them a story."

He seemed to consider this, then he nodded. "OK, it's one afternoon a week. I'll manage."

I shook my head. "There's another thing. I've decided I'm going to do more modelling. The work has been slowing up a bit recently, so I'm going to get it going again. I might have an early morning call, and you'll have to get them up, dressed and into school, too."

Leaving a slightly white-faced Barry standing in the kitchen, I grabbed my handbag and went straight out of the house. After slamming the door behind me, I stopped a moment on the step, taking a deep breath as I looked up and down Goldhurst Terrace. The neat rows of box hedges and tall trees lining the long road gave it the feeling of a lush green garden separating two rows of deep red brick houses. What was it making me feel? Was it freedom? Was it exhilaration? Maybe a bit of both.

Barry had had his fun. Now I was going to have mine.

My first stop that day was Leonard of Mayfair in Upper Grosvenor Street. Certainly it was one of the most fashionable and influential hair salons in London. I had decided it was the perfect place to create the new Annabelle. Famous people like Twiggy, Mick Jagger, Jean Shrimpton, and even Princess Margaret were clients. So if it was good enough for them...

"It's Mrs Gregory, isn't it?" Leonard said, coming up behind me as I got settled in the chair. "What are we looking for?"

"What do you recommend?" I asked.

"Hmm." He ran his fingers through my blonde curls, his dark eyes locked onto mine in the mirror. "Too wavy for the modern look." He shook his head. "I'm thinking a sculpted bob." He scratched the side of his impressively long nose. "With a full fringe."

"Colouring?" I asked.

"Oh, no." He shook his head. "You have a lovely colour. We'll keep it as it is."

"OK," I said with a smile. "Whatever you suggest, Leonard."

Two hours later, I walked out of the salon and made my way onto the street, my new sculpted bob brushing against my cheeks.

I made my way along Upper Grosvenor Street, down South Audley Street and onto Mount Street. My destination was the long-established fish restaurant called Scott's.

Arriving there only a few minutes after leaving Leonard's, I was met by the maître d'.

"You have a reservation, Madame?" he asked.

"I'm meeting someone," I explained. "Mrs Norton."

"Ahh. Bien sûr." He grabbed a menu. "Follow me, please."

Jilly was at a table for two, writing in a notebook. She closed it and put it down as I arrived. Once the maître d' had pulled my chair out so I could sit, and laid the napkin on my lap with a theatrical flourish, she gave me a broad smile.

"Lovely to see you, Annabelle," she said. "Looking good, too. Where did you get the hairdo?"

"Leonard's."

Her eyebrows raised. "Only the best!"

I smiled. "Thanks for seeing me, Jilly."

She nodded. "So what do I owe this get-together, Annabelle," she asked, then added quickly, "Not that it's not wonderful to see you, darling."

"I want to step up the modelling," I told her. "Do more."

She shrugged. "You're still getting assignments."

"I know. But not as much as before. The kids are growing up fast, and I've got the childcare sorted." The picture of a nonplussed Barry came to mind when I told him he'd have to take them to school. "I feel I can take on bigger assignments."

Jilly looked down as the waiter brought the drinks, and there was a pause in the conversation while we ordered. Once he'd gone, she cleared her throat. "The thing is, as your agent – of sorts – there's something I need to let you know. You're not a gamine teen or early twenty-something anymore, Annabelle." She bit her lip a moment. "It's getting harder to find work for someone your age."

"I don't want to stop," I said. "There are plenty of brands aimed at the older woman," I took a sip of my wine. "This is the 1970s, Jilly. There must be a call for girls my age." I shook my head. "And to be fair, I'm not that old. I'm thirty-two."

"I know, but the directors tend to want someone younger."

"Even for brands with an older profile?" I'd done my homework.

She gave this some consideration. "Fair point." She drummed her fingers on the table as she stared at me. "I've heard there's an Oil of Ulay ad shooting in Seefeld, Austria in two weeks." She nodded, as if she'd reached a decision. "The product's aimed at woman who are maybe late thirties or early forties. Your look could actually be just what they aspire to."

I gave her a smile. "That sounds perfect."

"We'll need updated headshots," Jilly continued, opening her notebook and scribbling. "And they'll want a test shoot with their photographer. I'll set it up." She closed the book and put it down. "You know, I've been thinking of you as a bit old for the younger brands. I suppose I'll have to swap that around." She smiled. "I'll see if I can get you work as a younger model for the older brands."

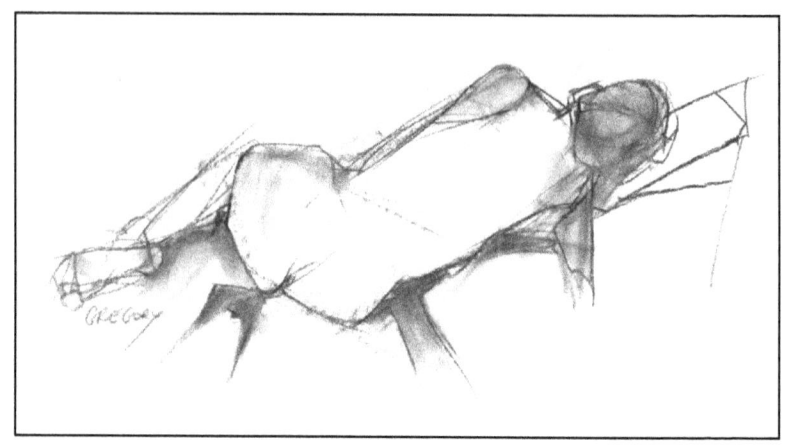

'Lying Nude'

Charcoal on paper. 42cm x 60cm.

My tutor at the Camden School of Art was Jack Yates.
This was one of the drawings I did for him.

Chapter Twenty-One

Becoming a Collage Artist, and a Hearse Driver

The life of the Gregory family settled into a fairly established routine after the reset in our marriage.

Jilly was as good as her word, and got me more modelling work for brands with an older profile. This started with a wonderful three days in Seefeld, shooting the Oil of Ulay ad on the snowy mountain slopes. As I first set foot in the village and gazed up in wonder at the majestic, towering peaks, my breath was truly taken away. There was the Seefelder Joch, the Seefelder Spitze, the Härmelekopf, and the highest of them all, the Reither Spitze; each one standing proudly and sharply defined against the deep blue sky. Had I found the beauty I had always sought? Certainly these mountains were breathtaking, with their sharp contrasts, snow-capped trees and craggy rocks. How very different from the ghastly alpine pictures painted by my great-grandfather in Whyteleafe!

I spent every moment away from the shoot walking around the village. Naturally my pad and pencils went everywhere with me, and I sketched every scene, wanting to capture the magnificence of the snowscape and the mountains. Although sadly none of the drawings I made seem to have survived.

Every Wednesday I spent the afternoon at the Camden School of Art, getting my fix of life drawing. Around fifteen of us would gather in the big studio, with the afternoon light filtering in through the tall windows. We would gather around our easels, our conversation muted as we prepared ourselves for the session. My routine consisted of several deep breaths and a conscious relaxing of my arms and legs. I didn't want any tension to get in the way of the drawing.

Our models were almost always fully nude. Jack Yates, the teacher, was insistent that we study the human form without any distractions of cloth or clothing. "Messes with the form and the shadows," he used to say. We often had a model called Susan, an unselfconscious woman in her forties who would stand on the raised platform, frequently in a natural pose, with her weight on one leg to create a relaxed twist to the upper body.

"I've been modelling at most of the art schools in London for years," she told me after class one afternoon, as we walked out onto Dalmeny Avenue heading for Camden Road. "It's a regular income and gives me plenty of time to think my own thoughts."

"It must be hard to keep still for so long," I said.

"The trick is to take regular breaks and relax the muscles," she answered.

"Oh gosh," I exclaimed. "I don't notice you taking any breaks."

"That's because I do it really quickly when as many people's heads are down as possible, then return to my original pose."

"How do you go back each time so accurately?" I genuinely thought she stayed still for the whole session – but it made sense that she would need to move occasionally.

"I have markers," she said. "Like an item in my line of vision." She stopped and turned to me, her face – that I knew so well – wearing an earnest expression. "Imagine there's a shelf, like the one in the studio, with pots of brushes and paints. I memorise the exact orientation of the contents; the way the brushes line up with each other, or the way a tube of paint is poking out. I get a fix on these, so I can return my head to the exact same angle by getting the orientation the same. And my body position then follows based on a small chalk mark I've made on the floor for my feet."

She walked on, leaving me standing in amazement. I had spent all my life being so focussed on developing my skills in capturing the beauty of the models, that I had not really thought about how skilled they were in being so still while we drew them.

I hurried after Susan, and we carried on chatting until we went our separate ways at the Camden Town tube station, and I took the underground home.

Jack Yates was not only a life drawing teacher, but he was also the reason why I started using collage as a medium in my art.

He came up to me as I was about to start packing up after a life class one evening.

"Annabelle, have you got a minute?"

"Sure," I replied, unsure as to what this might be about.

He pulled up a chair and sat by my easel. "I've been impressed with your work this term," he said, "and especially the way you see the model." He gestured at my drawing of Susan, half turned away, but with her face in profile looking back over her shoulder. "You're not just capturing what's actually there, but you're also finding the way the forms intersect and the shadows define them. How they overlap."

"Thanks," I said, giving him a sideways glance, still not sure where this was going.

"Have you ever tried collaging?" he asked. I shook my head. "You should. It fits with how your mind and eye work."

"How's that?"

"You like to build up your drawings in layers. You're not afraid to let one line interrupt another. That's an instinct that can be pushed even further with collaging."

He opened a book he'd been carrying and turned to a page that had a large abstract picture, mainly in green. As I looked, the image of a seated man seemed to emerge. It was created out of many layers of geometric shapes, so hadn't been immediately obvious. I found its very obscurity intriguing.

"This is *Tomorrow I May Be Far Away* by Romare Bearden," Jack said. "See how he's cut out elements from magazines and newspapers, and laid them over the painted background to create the image?"

I took the book and studied the picture carefully. The more I looked, the more details emerged. The image was created by the cuttings; their shape as well as their colour giving it an unexpected complexity. I loved how the positioning of the paper pieces created not just the actual shapes, but the suggestion of lines and images. Was that a face and a hand in the top left? A garden in the background with a fence? Maybe a woman and a tree?

"It's not about cutting out and pasting bits of paper," Jack continued. "It's about having an eye for how shapes relate to each other; how diverse elements create a different image through their relative positions."

"I love it," I said. "How it changes if you look from a distance, compared to close-up. I wouldn't need to worry about getting the proportions right – I can just compose it as a free-form picture."

"It's a whole new visual language, Annabelle," Jack said. "A whole new way of bringing your composition skills to life." I handed the book back and he stood. "Stay on after life drawing next week; I have a collaging class following this one. You can give it a try."

I told Barry when I got home that I was going to be out even longer each week at the school.

"You'll need to give the kids their supper, bathe and put them to bed," I said. "You can cook them something nice. Be a good husband and father."

He gave a weak smile, seeming to know that I still had him on the back foot. He had never mentioned the affair again, but I found myself unable to stop making occasional caustic allusions to it. When your trust in someone is destroyed, it's very hard – if not impossible – to get it back.

Do I believe he was never unfaithful again? Maybe. Maybe not. In truth, I found the best way to cope was to throw myself into looking after my kids, creating my art, modelling, and trying as best I could to put such questions out of my mind. That way the marriage and family life was able to continue.

This situation also forced Barry to be more of a hands-on father to the children; something he seemed to find a challenge initially, but then he settled into it as the circumstances demanded. As he became more in tune with their needs, I couldn't help seeing the contrast with my own father's shortcomings as a parent. This was brought painfully to light as Christmas approached, when I got a totally unexpected letter from him.

I saw the envelope on the hall table one morning and thought I vaguely recognised the handwriting. Idly, I turned it over, but there was no real clue who had sent it. Barry came down the stairs.

"Do you know who this is from?" I asked.

"There is an easy way to find out," he suggested. "Open it?"

I gave a small tut and sigh, as if to say I knew that, but just wanted to involve him in the discussion. I opened it and took out a single-sided hand-written note.

Dear Annabelle
I thought I would like to come and see you for an afternoon and meet my grandchildren. Would Sunday next be appropriate? At 2 p.m.?
Yours sincerely,
Thomas Sylvester (your father)

Once I had got over the excruciating formality, and the apparent need to be reminded of our relationship, I decided it was possibly a good thing – mainly to enable the children to meet him. Perhaps after all these years he had mellowed? Maybe he could become a part of their lives; the grandpa they'd often asked about but never actually met.

He arrived at 2 p.m. the following Sunday and was greeted by three excited children. They had been preparing for the visit ever since I informed them their Grandpa was coming. They had decided that they would each give him a special gift, and there was much discussion and debate as to what these would be. In the event, each child found something they thought he would like. Marcus found a book on circuses, Wayne bought a toy Fiat Multipla, which he painted black and white after I told him that was the colour of my father's taxis, and Sacha settled for a box of chocolates. "Everyone likes chocolates," she said, with an air of expertise on the matter. "He'll love them."

Each present was carefully wrapped and a card taped on, with a suitable greeting from the grandchild concerned. I'd baked a cake and had tea ready when he arrived.

My father looked smaller and older than I expected: a rather dour little man in a slightly shabby suit and overcoat. I'd hardly seen him since he'd let me down by not speaking at the wedding, but I was prepared to let bygones be bygones and give him a chance.

"Hello Annabelle," he said, as I took his coat and hat, then showed him into the living room. Three well-scrubbed faces lit up when he came in, and they clustered round him, bombarding him with questions, which he seemed to struggle to answer.

Eventually there was calm, and tea and cakes were served. I asked him what he'd been doing.

"Oh a bit of this and a bit of that," he replied, his eyes anywhere but on me.

"Are you still running the taxis?" I asked.

"No, that folded a couple of years ago. The black cabs really have London sewn up now."

There was more non-committal conversation, until Sacha ran to the Christmas tree, and picked out her present. "Here you are, Grandpa," she said in a breathless voice. "Happy Christmas." Marcus and Wayne each gave him their presents, and there was a moment of childish anticipation as they watched him open the gifts, make slightly vague expressions of gratitude, then put them in a pile beside the chair.

After an hour or so of chat, he seemed to feel as if he'd done his duty and made a move to go. The children said goodbye and went up to their rooms, while I saw him to the hall and gave him his hat and coat. Then, with a vague promise to 'keep in touch', he left.

It was only that evening, when I went into the living room to tidy up, that I saw the pile of presents he had left.

Unforgivable.

☙❧

Now that Barry was not tied to a restaurant or club for sixteen hours a day, his natural entrepreneurial spirit started to shine through. As a dealer, he would buy and sell whatever caught his fancy. It was not just antiques and paintings; what had also caught his fancy, were high-end luxury cars.

He and a man called Robert Dawson set up a motor trade business in Lambourne Place in South East London. They bought and sold cars – mainly Bentleys and Rolls-Royces, but other makes as well. Barry wasn't too picky; if he thought he could make a quick sale (or a 'flip' as he called it), he would buy the car, give it whatever refurbishment it needed, and sell it on.

Perhaps it was my father and his 'taxi wars', or the time when Annie and I were nearly lured into a horrid old man's car sales caravan, but I have always had a somewhat jaundiced view of motor cars. Yes, they give you freedom: the opportunity to travel, to see the natural beauty of the world. But at heart they're really just a means to an end. They get you from A to B in some level of comfort and that is a good thing, but I don't understand men's obsession with them. Particularly with how fast they go. I do like the fact they can go fast when you want them to (I'm told that for a woman in her eighties, I do drive quite quickly – but that's not the point I'm making here). It's the constant talking about it that leaves me cold. I mean, even the cheapest runabout nowadays can keep up a constant seventy miles an hour on the motorway. So why do you need all that speed? And why on earth do you need to make a car *look* as if it goes very fast?

But like so many men, Barry was concerned with all aspects of the cars he bought and sold. This had some effect on me, as I usually had to use these vehicles as runabouts until he sold them. My Alfa Romeo had gone by this time, as it had simply stopped working one day for no apparent reason. I had become used to getting to know each new car as he brought it home, getting to understand its idiosyncrasies and foibles. And there were plenty of these; in the early 1970s cars were temperamental beasts. They would sometimes refuse to start, or they might overheat, or there might be any number of other problems. There was the Austin Allegro with its large square steering wheel that left bruises on my thighs whenever I turned a corner. Or the Porsche 924 that would only agree to start on warm dry days.

Then there was the Humber hearse.

Barry brought it home one day, beeping the horn outside, so that Marcus, Wayne, Sacha and I felt obliged to come out and take a look.

And what a sight it was.

It was one of those big black hearses you often see heading up funeral processions, usually with 'Mum', 'Dad', 'Nan' or something similar written in flowers visible through the windows. It had a wide chrome grille and four round headlights.

But what really caught the eye was the way it had been modified. The wheels were large and made of smooth polished metal, while the sides had been painted with bright red, yellow and orange flames. They started just behind the front wheels, then fanned out up the doors and towards where the coffin would rest in the back. The whole effect looked totally bizarre.

"What do you think?" Barry asked, after he had clambered out and come to stand beside his open-mouthed family.

"What... on... earth...?" I began, then spluttered to a stop. "What on earth," I tried again, "possessed you to buy such a monstrosity?"

"It was boring and black when I bought it. I thought it could do with a bit of livening up."

"You mean – it was *you* who had it painted?"

"Yes," he laughed. "It's a bit of fun!"

"Barry," I whispered. "It's got flames up the side!"

"Yeah, a subversive hot-rod hearse!"

"Cool, Dad," Wayne agreed.

"But... flames!" I stared at his smiling face. "With a coffin... It's as if it's trying to be a..." I could hardly say it. "...a mobile crematorium."

He made a dismissive gesture with his hand. "Subversive. There'll be some popstar or boxer or somesuch who'll love it. Didn't you see John Lennon's Rolls a few years back? He painted it all over with psychedelic patterns! And the Americans go mad for these. They add massive engines and paint jobs like this to hearses all the time."

"But... that's America, Barry. This is London."

"Don't worry Annabelle. I'll sell it, you'll see."

"But... what will you do with it in the meantime?"

His smile broadened. "We'll use it ourselves."

I was left speechless at this. To use a vehicle like this as a school run car... my blood ran cold. To turn up at the school gates in a mobile crematorium... Then I spotted a possible way out. "It's got no back seats. I won't get all the kids in."

"No, this one's got a bench seat in the front. Plenty of room if they squash in. You'll be fine."

My mouth snapped shut. This was the only vehicle we now had. What choice had I got?

The following morning, I stood with the three kids in their school uniforms, as we contemplated the hearse.

"Mum, I want to lie on the platform in the back." This was Wayne.

"You can't," I said, "what if I have to brake suddenly? You'll be thrown around like a pea in a drum. I don't want you killed."

He shrugged. "Then you can drive me straight to the cemetery."

"Don't be silly. Squeeze in, all of you."

For the next couple of weeks we were the figures of fun as we drove slowly through West London, and particularly when we were at the school. Suddenly everyone was a comedian.

"You're clearly in a hurry to get to the afterlife!"

"Do the flames make it go faster, or just burn through petrol?"

And the one we heard the most; "I wouldn't be seen dead in that."

One afternoon, we were heading home from school, and as I had become a bit more used to the hearse, I was driving it a little faster. It also had power steering that was quite light, so it had a tendency to turn a bit too eagerly. I was heading up a line of parked cars, when a van suddenly appeared from a side street. With a scream I threw the steering to the right. The van screeched to a halt, and we avoided it by inches. Then I looked at where we were heading and screamed again. We were careering across the oncoming traffic. Cars coming the other way were hitting their brakes and skidding to a halt. It was a miracle none of them crashed into us.

But now the hearse was heading straight for a red post box.

There was nothing I could do.

With a heart-stopping crunch and the noise of metal scraping on metal, the car hit the post box and came to a stop.

For a moment there was silence, as I struggled to take in the enormity of what had just happened.

Peeling my hands off the wheel with difficulty, I looked across at three wide-eyed white faces beside me. "You OK, kids?" I whispered. There were three nods, and I let out a sigh of relief.

"Put it in reverse, Mum," Marcus said.

I did as he suggested, and there was a grinding noise as the hearse parted from the post box.

I switched it off and we all got out and looked at the damage, which surprisingly was not as bad as I thought it would be. The grille of the hearse was a bit bent in, and there was a large black mark on the post box, although it didn't seem to be damaged structurally. "Those boxes are pretty sturdy," Marcus observed. "But we'll need to report it," he added.

"Maybe the postman will be along soon," said Wayne, pointing at the small white sign below the letterbox slot. "It says the post will be collected at 5 p.m. That's in half an hour."

I looked across at the building next to us, which was a pub. "Come on kids," I said, "We'll wait in there."

I moved the car off the pavement and parked it by the side of the road, and we all trooped into the pub. The girl behind the bar looked at three under-age children and seemed about to say something about them not being allowed in the pub, but I said, "We've just crashed our hearse into the post box outside. We need to come in and recover ourselves."

I'm not sure which part of what I said shocked her the most: the crash bit, or the fact we were driving a hearse. But whatever it was, she let us stay, even serving the kids with glasses of orange juice.

Wayne, who'd been watching at the window, alerted us when the postman turned up. I went out and gave the man our details, and he seemed pretty sanguine about it. "Don't look like too much damage, love," he said, as he put the post in his sack. "I'll report it, but I don't think there'll be much to pay."

He looked at the hearse, parked on the road. "Course, can't say the same for your hearse, love. Who you married to? Count Dracula?" With a chuckle, he picked up his sack, got in his van and drove off.

Count Dracula, otherwise known as Barry Gregory, also saw the funny side. "You wrapped it round a post box?" he laughed. "That's priceless!"

I felt he was missing the point. "We are all OK, Barry," I told him. "Thanks for asking."

He nodded. "That's good." He paused. "But I have a buyer, so I'll need to get it repaired. I'll take it to the garage tomorrow."

"How am I going to get the kids to school?" I demanded.

"Oh, that's no problem. I've got something else coming." Shortly after there was the deep note of a horn from outside. "That'll be the new car," he said.

"It had better not be another hearse," I muttered as we went to the door. "It's been so embarrassing at the schools. This one needs to be something ordinary."

But Barry had a strange look on his face, as if he was hiding something from me. I stopped in the hall. "What is it, Barry?" I said. "It had better not be anything really embarrassing, like a Rolls-Royce. I don't want people thinking we're trying to be posh..."

He drew a sharp breath. "Sorry love," he said, opening the front door.

Outside was an enormous car with a Spirit of Ecstasy on the bonnet.

"It's a Silver Cloud," he said. "Please try not to wrap this one round a post box."

Marcus

Pencil on paper.

Marcus watching the TV.

Chapter Twenty-Two

Becoming an Understanding Mother

My search for the true meaning of beauty has been a constant theme in this memoir, running through it like the lead that runs through a pencil. There have been times when I think I might have found it, such as in the mountains at Seefeld. Or maybe it has been revealed to me in the people like Susan who have modelled in life classes, as I do my best to capture the softness of their curves, the form of their muscles, or even the fall of their hair over bare shoulders. But above all I am a mother, and you'll not be surprised if I say there is no moment more beautiful than the first time you gaze on the scrunched up little features of your newborn baby.

Each of the three times I've held my new child, it's been a beautiful, if different, experience.

I was a nervous twenty-two-year-old when I first rocked Marcus in my arms, petrified by the new responsibility that I must now take on.

As a slightly more experienced twenty-three-year-old, I held Wayne. With all I had now learned, I was much better prepared, and with that I found more confidence.

Then, four years later, Sacha came along, and my heart swelled with pride as I gazed down into the bright blue eyes of my own little girl.

There's so much potential, so much hope and expectation as you hold each little bundle. As you trace a finger across each perfect little forehead, down each little button nose, across each little pair of rosebud lips. What will they do with their lives? What kind of personality will they have? So many possibilities, all contained in this one, beautiful little human.

Marcus grew into a charmer – good with his hands as well as his brain: a soldier, an electrician, a building surveyor.

Wayne was always a free spirit – a wild child who grew into an adventurous young man. Maybe that was a result of my own increasing confidence when he was born – no longer the nervous new mother. I was more ready to let him do what he wanted; to let him follow in his older brother's footsteps.

Then there was Sacha – my beautiful, beautiful girl. So bright, so positive. My friend and companion as much as my daughter. Sacha should have had such a wonderful life. She should have had everything to live for. Everything to achieve.

She should have.

※

The island of Alderney has always played a large part in my life, and that of the whole family. From the time I first went there with Miss Palmer and her Junior Naturalist Club, to our regular family holidays, the island has been something of a second home. Which is why in 1977, Barry and I decided to go there for a special trip; one where we could look at houses, to see if we could buy one and move out of London. To be honest, it was a bit of a dream; we had no idea how we would live and earn an income on the island, but we thought we would have a look all the same.

We felt it should just be the two of us going, as we would be spending our days traipsing around viewings rather than having family time. Which left the question of who would look after the kids while we were away.

"I'll do it," Marcus announced when we broached the subject one evening. "I'm over fourteen, so I am legally allowed."

"Actually, that's not the case," Barry pointed out. "We can leave you in charge, but if anything happens, until you're sixteen we're technically responsible."

"But it'll be fine," Marcus protested. "You know you can trust me."

Despite some misgivings on my part, we finally gave in, and Marcus was left in charge of the house and his siblings; twelve-year-old Wayne and nine-year-old Sacha.

We went away for the week, driving first down to Southampton, where we caught the Aurigny Airline flight direct to Alderney.

The flight was in an old propeller aircraft, which not only rattled your teeth on take-off and landing, but while it was in the air as well. Once we had levelled out from the climb, Barry decided to reach for a cigarette. He had just lit it and blown out a puff of smoke, when the stewardess came rushing up.

"You can't smoke, sir," she snapped. "Please put it out."

Barry indicated the 'no smoking' sign, which was unlit. "The sign's off," he pointed out. "Which means I can smoke."

"No sir," she replied. "Smoking is not allowed on the flight at any time." She paused, looking at Barry with the kind of sneer I suspected wouldn't be found in her training manual. "Did you not listen to the safety announcement? It's been completely banned on this airline for over two months now."

"No smoking on a flight?" Barry asked, his voice flat with disbelief.

"That's right, sir," the stewardess said. "Aurigny is the first and only airline to ban smoking on all its flights."

Eventually Barry stubbed it out and sat back in his seat with arms folded. "That's a ruddy nuisance," he observed. "A fag calms my nerves in this rattle-can of a plane."

"If it's banned, it's banned," I said, then couldn't stop myself adding with a stern tone in my voice, "it's about following the rules, Barry. As you should know."

Seeming either to have misunderstood my implied reference back to his Cloggy woman, or simply ignoring it, he said, "Annabelle, did *you* hear them say there's no smoking when they did the announcement?"

"No," I had to admit, forcing myself back to the thrust of the conversation. "But I tend to tune those things out anyway." I'd flown so many times since that memorable first flight to Saint-Tropez, that I really didn't hear the safety briefings any more.

"Talking of following rules," he continued. "Do you think Marcus will be OK looking after Wayne and Sacha?"

"I do hope so," I said. "It's his first try at being totally responsible."

"Will he have enough food?"

"I filled the freezer not long ago," I replied. "There's more than enough in there for a month, let alone a week."

The flight rattled on, landing shortly after at Alderney Airport.

We looked at ten or twelve houses on the island, but none really caught our fancy. They were either too small or too large, too expensive or too shabby, too isolated or too surrounded. In the end, we decided to abandon our dream of country living on the island.

"We'll just have to keep coming here on holiday," Barry suggested, once we were back in the air on the way home.

I said nothing, as I struggled with mixed emotions. On the one hand, I was disappointed we hadn't found anything. I loved Alderney, and the thought of having a place of our own in its glorious countryside was a dream I was reluctant to give up. More and more I was realising that I no longer felt settled in London. My sister, Ingrid, had a charming cottage in the Oxfordshire countryside, and whenever I went there, I felt an incredible sense of peace. It was not just that I loved to paint the natural world, it was that I was more and more finding the heat and the smoke of London was stifling me.

We landed back in Southampton and drove home.

The house was an absolute bombsite.

If Barry had left it a mess when we were in Cumbria, the kids left it worse. A whole lot worse.

The hallway looked as if all three children had used it as a dressing room. There were shoes, socks, pants, trousers, a couple of dresses and a skirt tossed all round, as if a laundry basket had exploded. Both dresses and some of the socks had been flung over the bannisters – whether by accident or design, I had no idea.

Wordlessly, Barry and I picked our way through the debris and stepped cautiously into the kitchen.

It was as bad as I might have feared.

There were piles of dishes stacked in and around the sink, many with what looked like an old red scab squeezing out between them. I suspected this was dried ketchup, but I was reluctant to touch it and find out. Several saucepans were on the stove, one with what looked suspiciously like burned baked beans stuck to the bottom, and which would probably never come off. I made a mental note to get new pans.

The worktop looked like it had been caught in an Angel Delight snowstorm, with three empty packets lying on top of a liberal dusting of powder. Nearby was a mixing bowl that had three spoons glued to the insides by sticky caked-on mousse. The electric hand blender lay on its side nearby, with both stainless steel whisks still in place. Spots of dried-on spatter spread around the bowl, on the worktop, the cooker and even on the kitchen cabinets several feet away. The whisks hadn't been cleaned, as there was still dried-on Angel Delight on the inside of the blades. Two empty milk bottles were also in evidence. It wouldn't take an expert crime-scene investigator to reconstruct what had taken place; three children each emptying their packet into the bowl, pouring in two pints of milk, then whisking it into a multi-flavoured pudding, before standing round the bowl with a spoon each, gobbling it all down. Someone had then licked the whisks clean, but only on the outside of each blade.

With a deep sigh I left this scene of devastation, eased the fridge door open and peered in. It was virtually empty; just half a lemon, a brown-leafed lettuce and a single wrinkled potato.

I went through to the utility room and lifted the lid of the chest freezer. As I'd told Barry, it had been full to the brim when we'd left a week ago.

Like the fridge, it was almost completely empty, save for a single packet at the bottom. I peered in; it was fish fingers. I grabbed it and gave a small grunt of surprise. It had no weight at all, so that when I shook it, the flap flipped open, and a small shower of fish finger crumbs sprayed out. They'd taken the contents and put the empty packet back in the freezer.

"We've been eaten out of house and home," Barry observed from over my shoulder.

I closed the freezer and stepped back.

"Where's Marcus?" I growled. "We need to talk."

Barry and I went upstairs, to find the three children gathered in Wayne's room, each with a look of studied innocence carefully applied to their faces.

I put my hands on my hips. "Marcus Gregory..." I began.

Marcus gave me a dazzling smile, got up and threw his arms around me. "Hello, Mum," he said. "It's so lovely to see you back. You're looking very well; the fresh Alderney air must have been so good for you after the stuffiness of London. Did you and Dad have a good time together? Did you find a house?"

I looked over his shoulder. Little Sacha gave us a smile as well. "We've had such a lovely time, Mummy," she said. "Marcus has looked after us so well."

Wayne joined in. "We've cooked all our own meals, Mum," he said, while Marcus hugged me even tighter, as if he was trying to squeeze me into submission. "We've learned so much about making meals," Wayne continued. "We might have made a bit of a mess, Mum, but we'll clear it up. Promise."

The cheek of it was a work of art. What could I possibly say?

Wayne

Pencil on paper.

Two studies of my middle son.

Chapter Twenty-Three

Becoming Intrigued By My Son's Resourcefulness

It was a couple of years after this that that Wayne built himself a sailing boat.

I was making supper one evening (spaghetti Bolognese, if I remember rightly), when my eye was caught by the end of a large piece of wood appearing to float down the corridor beyond the open kitchen door. I paused, my knife in mid-air above the onion I was chopping. A moment later, Wayne staggered into view, balancing the wood on his shoulder.

He stopped and caught my eye. "What on earth are you doing?" I asked. "What's that you've got?"

"It's a keel," he informed me. "For the boat I'm making."

"I beg your pardon? What boat?"

"I thought I'd make one."

"A proper boat?" I said. "Not a model? One you can sit in?"

"Of course," he replied, with a dismissive toss of his head, as if having to explain something so obvious was quite beneath him. "What's the point of building a boat if you can't get in it?"

"Where are you building it?"

"On the patio in the back garden."

"I see. And where are the bits coming from?"

"My friend Kenneth's dad bought a kit, but he hasn't got time to build it himself, so he let me have it."

"I see." I gave the onion another cut while I considered this. "And have you paid for it?"

"Yeah. I gave him a hundred quid for it."

"Wayne," I said, "you're fourteen-years-old. Where on earth did you get that much money?"

He gave a small shrug and shifted the keel on his shoulder. "A few odd jobs for Dad, some things I've found down at the river bank, and a few other bits and bobs."

"Things?" I asked, unable to keep the suspicion out of my voice. "What things? And what bits and bobs?"

Marcus came in behind his brother, carrying another piece of wood. "He's been grubbing around in the mud by the Thames at London Bridge," he told me, taking over the conversation as Wayne carried on down the corridor. "He found some posy rings and did a deal with a museum."

"Posy rings?" I repeated, conscious that I sounded a bit dim by repeating everything.

"Yeah. A couple of ceramic ones, and some antique ones. One had engraving inside and everything. I think he got £100 for that one alone. And quite a few coins – some really old. A couple of them are Roman, according to the guy at the museum."

I pondered this. Wayne's clothes had frequently had mud on them, but I thought he'd just been playing in the park.

"And he said, 'bits and bobs' as well," I queried.

"Yeah." Marcus grinned. "He's been going up onto Hampstead Heath, and searching the bushes where the queers go to..." As I stared at him with my mouth hanging open, Marcus explained, "When they drop their trousers, all their loose change falls out." He walked a couple of steps further, then stopped and looked back over his shoulder.

"There's gold in them thar hills," he added in an American accent.

Over the next few weeks, the boat took shape, with Barry and I watching from the sitting room as the boys sawed, nailed and painted the upturned hull. They even let Sacha join in, giving her jobs to do, and congratulating her when she completed the work successfully. Eventually the hull was turned over, and Barry and I came out to admire it.

The boat was about eight feet long, with a wooden seat across the middle and a crossbeam towards the front. "It's called the 'bow', Mum," Wayne informed me. The crossbeam had a hole, which Wayne told us was to take the mast. At the back – or the 'stern' – there was a large, hinged board attached to a piece of wood that enabled the boys to steer. "Crikey, Mum. It's the 'rudder' and the 'tiller'. Come on, get with the programme."

On the back, they had painted *Xerxes* in gold lettering.

"Xerxes?" I enquired.

"The king of Persia who beat the Spartans at the Battle of Thermopylae."

"I see." Quite how that was connected to a boat in West London, I wasn't sure. But I let it go and gave *Xerxes* a closer inspection. They seemed to have done a very professional job. It's very good, boys," I said. "Where will you sail it?"

"We'll take it to the Thames," Wayne informed me. "Dad said he can put it on the roof of the van."

"I see." I put my hand on my chin. "It's extremely fortunate we have one of the very few semi-detached houses in the whole of Goldhurst Terrace. Otherwise the only way you would have got it out would have been by crane over the roof."

I was in the kitchen an hour or so later, when I heard a series of shouts from the back patio. It sounded like instructions were being given then countermanded. I put down my knife and went out to see what it was all about.

Barry and the two boys were standing around the boat, hands on hips and mouths in tight lines.

"What's the matter?" I asked, putting a casual, de-escalatory note into my voice.

"The passageway is very narrow," Barry pointed across to the side of the house, his voice strained. "Not much wider than the hull on its side. The boys and I have different ideas as to how best to carry the boat out."

"Dad says we should tie ropes to the bow and stern and carry it out that way," Marcus explained. "But Wayne and me, we think it will be much easier if we lift it onto our shoulders."

"Until it overbalances, and hits a wall," muttered Barry.

"It's our boat, Dad," Wayne said. "Let us decide."

There was a long pause, and I couldn't help thinking it was like a Sergio Leone movie standoff scene, with the camera cutting to each one in turn. Marcus – defiant, his brow furrowed. Wayne – observant, his eyes flicking from his father to his brother. Barry – coming to the realisation he was no longer the unquestioned authority-figure.

Barry stood back. "OK, boys," he said through gritted teeth. "Do it your way."

The boys hefted *Xerxes* onto their shoulders and walked it through the passageway, getting it to the other end with only minor damage to a drainpipe.

Once they had lifted it onto the roof of the van, Barry absolutely insisted on strapping it down himself. "It's one thing taking out a drainpipe, but it's another causing a major road accident," he muttered, as he pulled on the straps until they were tight enough.

Barry also checked with the Port of London Authority regarding registration. Apparently it wasn't necessary, but the boys did have to have insurance (in case they hit an expensive gin-palace, and there were plenty of those). He insisted they wore lifejackets, even though, according to Wayne, they weren't compulsory.

Xerxes had a fairly happy few years being sailed mainly by Wayne. Sometimes he sailed on his own, but once or twice he took Sacha, who seemed thrilled to be having time with her brother. Eventually it was sold to someone at a local sailing club, and I have no doubt they had as much fun in it as my own kids did.

Sacha

Pencil on paper.

My beautiful daughter.

Chapter Twenty-Four

Becoming The Cause Of A Teenage Tantrum

When Sacha first sat on a pony, it was clear that she was destined to be a natural horsewoman. Her love of horses grew almost as fast as she did, and like so many obsessed little girls, she spent as much of her time as possible riding horses and caring for them.

When she wasn't in school, Barry or I would take her to her favourite place, a riding school in Hampstead. Sacha would spend weekends and summer evenings riding through the park with the instructors, then she would help with the care of the horses; mucking them out, brushing them down and making sure they had a bag of oats and water in their troughs. In the car on the way home, I would get a blow-by-blow account of the afternoon's equestrian activities, until I felt I could not only identify every one of the ponies by its name, colour, size and temperament, but I could then conduct a guided tour of each of their stables.

By the time Sacha was in her mid-teens, Barry and I decided we'd finally had enough of the smoke and noise of London. The earlier aborted attempt to find a place on Alderney had been a dream, but now it became clear we had to turn it into reality. I mentioned earlier that my sister, Ingrid, had a place in Oxfordshire, in a little village near Banbury. It was when Sacha and I were staying with her for a summer's weekend that the idea for a move to Oxfordshire crystallised.

We were in Ingrid's garden in the sunshine. I lay back on the sun lounger and wriggled my toes. "This is bliss," I observed. "No noisy cars, no smoke, no grime. Just peace." I took a sip of white wine while a wood pigeon gave its distinctive five-note call from one of the birch trees; the soundtrack to the countryside.

"Why don't you leave London, then?" Ingrid asked. "Move to the country?"

"We want to," I said, with a wistful smile. "But it never seems to be the right time."

Ever since Barry and I had failed to find a house on Alderney, we had resigned ourselves to staying in London – and the ties to the city had become ever stronger. The antiques business had grown, and we still did the market in Hampstead every weekend. Barry had taken the lease on some old stables in Camden, and had been restoring furniture and paintings from there. Marcus had been helping his father out, until he left home to join the army. And Barry's car business was also thriving.

I gave an involuntary shudder; the memory of the hearse crunching into the post box was all too painful. And then the stares and laughter as we drove to school for the next couple of weeks in that awful old Rolls Royce.

Then there was his art restoration business. That Allan Ramsey Barry had got from the clearance in Campden Hill Road had been the first of many such paintings, and his restoration course in Wales had paid itself back many times over. I'd taken to giving him an encouraging smile whenever he told me he'd sold some art. And while I knew the vast majority of his deals were kosher, I also knew he wasn't above bending the rules a bit if it brought in a few extra quid. Marcus had let slip one time that when a customer had picked up an antique painting, the signature was still wet.

"We've got too many ties to London." I gave a small sigh. "Sacha's school is another thing; she's got her O-Levels coming up soon."

"And all my friends are in London, Auntie Ingrid," Sacha added from the lounger beyond. "Sophie, Izzy, Bella and me; we're always round each other's houses, revising."

"I see." Ingrid was quiet a moment, and I could see she was mulling all this over. Then she said, "Of course, you could always find a new school; a bright girl like you would make lots of new friends." She turned over and leant across to me. "Barry's business can transfer to the country. It's not like London is the only place where antiques and cars can be bought and sold. Oxford's pretty busy in that department, too. And you can easily get to London each weekend for the market; it's only an hour and a half from here. Even less first thing in the morning at the weekend."

I didn't answer immediately. My mind was whirring as I considered the obstacles, and realised that, with a bit of thought and application, we could actually overcome each one. Ingrid was right. If we planned ahead – and were prepared to accept some changes – we could make it work.

"Mum!" Sacha sat up and gave me a shocked look. "You're not actually thinking about it, are you? You're not seriously going to make us leave London?"

"I don't know, Sacha love," I replied. "Maybe."

"Oh, Mum!" she yelped as she leapt up off the sun lounger, then stomped across the patio and disappeared into the house. There was a silence from me and Ingrid as we watched her go.

"She'll come round," Ingrid observed. "If you do really want to move?"

The wood pigeon gave its throaty call. The trees rustled quietly in the summer breeze. Other than that there was total quiet. Total peace. What a beautiful thing.

"Yes," I said. "We're going to leave London and live in the country.

Sacha sat with her arms folded in bristling silence as we drove back that evening. It was a silence that had lasted ever since she had flounced into Ingrid's house, apart from a few monosyllabic grunts at supper in response to polite questions from the grown-ups. Her frown and tight lips seemed to get worse the closer we got to London, as if flood waters were building up behind a dam.

Eventually, somewhere around Wembley, the dam burst.

"I cannot *believe* it!" she snapped suddenly, and I had to stop myself swerving in surprise. "I cannot *believe* you're even *thinking* of leaving London!"

Pleased that we were at least talking again, I steadied the car and said, "It's only an idea, Sacha love."

"But you want to. I know it."

"Well, yes. I am finding London grey, smelly, and dirty. I want to be enjoying the beauty of the country, not staring at brick walls."

"But I'm not leaving my friends."

"There are things such as telephones, trains and letters," I pointed out. "You can stay in touch very easily nowadays." I paused as I overtook a van, then added, "And you'll make new friends as well. It's a win-win."

"No Mum," she said, before giving the perennial cry of the teenager, "it's not *fair!*"

We got back to Goldhurst Terrace without much more conversation. As soon as I parked, she got out and marched into the house. I followed her in, just in time to see her stomping up the stairs. She disappeared into her bedroom with a house-shaking door slam.

In the sitting room, Barry looked up from his newspaper with a raised eyebrow. "What was that all about?"

I explained the whole situation, and how Sacha had taken it.

He put the newspaper down. "I see. And you think if we sold this place, it's Oxfordshire where we should go?"

"Yes, Barry, I do."

"Hmm... OK then."

"Oh," I gasped. "You mean it?"

"Yeah. I've been finding it all a bit much since we first thought of moving out of London, truth be told. Work's been quite hectic since Marcus left, what with all the different businesses I'm running. And Wayne's not been any good; I never know where he is from one minute to the next."

"We can find somewhere near Ingrid. Near Banbury," I said, my voice rising with excitement. "And we'll have to put this house on the market."

"Sure," Barry agreed. "And find a school for Sacha to do her A-Levels."

"Oh God," I groaned, sinking into a chair as the full impact of my daughter's disappointment made my excitement deflate like a burst balloon. "She'll never forgive me for taking her away from London."

In the event, she was finally reconciled to leaving Sophie, Izzy and Bella when she first stepped into the charming little cottage we bought in the Oxfordshire village of Deddington. She found a local riding stables and settled into country life more readily than she probably thought she would.

The move was also a good thing because it brought us closer to the John Radcliffe hospital in Oxford. A place we later found we would have to visit for regular treatment.

For a tumour in her brain.

Photo of me and Sacha

This was taken on a visit to Deddington Castle, near our cottage when we moved out of London to Oxfordshire.

Chapter Twenty-Five

Becoming A Hospital Mother

As a mother, there is nothing that tears at your soul more than seeing your beautiful child suffering a devastating illness.

It all started one day when we had been in Deddington for a few months, living in the lovely little cottage we had found.

We were driving back from the riding stables one evening when Sacha put her hands to her temples as if trying to rub away pain.

"I feel funny, Mummy," she said. "And I couldn't feel my left hand properly when I was riding. It was as if it was all tingly, but numb."

I found a packet of paracetamol when we got home, and suggested she go to bed and rest. "It's probably just tiredness," I said, as I gave her a glass of water and a couple of tablets. "You've been doing a lot recently, what with revising for your exams and going riding. Take these and I'm sure you'll feel better in the morning."

She took the tablets, then said, "Actually, the headaches seem worse in the mornings."

"Oh," I exclaimed. "Have you been getting them for a while?"

She nodded, wide-eyed.

"Why didn't you tell me?"

"I didn't think anything of it."

That all changed the next morning, when I had breakfast on the table and called up to Sacha. There was no answer, but I thought I heard what sounded like prolonged retching from the bathroom.

I ran up and pushed open the door, to find her kneeling in front of the toilet. She looked up, her eyes red. I handed her a towel, and she wiped her mouth.

"It's got sick on it now," she said, trying a weak smile as she handed it back.

"It can be washed," I replied. "And I'm taking you to the doctor, young lady."

A few hours later we were sitting in the waiting room at the Deddington Health Centre. Sacha pressed her hand against her temple.

"Still got the headache?" I asked.

She nodded, then shook her left hand. "And the funny feeling in my hand," she said.

"I'm sure it's nothing," I said, as much to reassure myself as her. "Probably just growing pains." But somehow, I had a sick feeling of my own, a feeling that it was something worse. Much worse.

I took a deep breath, then gave Sacha my most reassuring smile. "We'll see the doctor, and she'll give you some pills, and you'll be better in no time."

Before Sacha could reply, a voice called out, "Sacha Gregory?" A blonde woman in her late thirties wearing a cardigan, tweed skirt and flat shoes was standing in the doorway. We followed her into the consulting room. "What seems to be the matter?" she asked, once Sacha and I had sat beside the desk.

I wanted to point out that 'seems' suggested as if it was all in Sacha's head. Which, of course, was exactly where it was – but we didn't know that at the time.

Sacha explained her symptoms.

"And how long has this been happening?"

"A few weeks. Five or six, maybe."

The doctor looked at me, as if to ask why I had let this go on for such a long time. Sacha said quickly, "I only told Mum yesterday."

"I see. And these headaches? Describe them."

"A dull ache in the mornings," Sacha paused and rubbed her temple. "They're not terrible, just... always there. Sometimes they go on all day. And I've been sick a few times."

"I see," the doctor said, scribbling notes. "Anything else?"

Sacha held up her left hand, flexing the fingers. "It goes funny sometimes. Like pins and needles, but not quite. Tingly."

The doctor stood up. "Let's have a look at you then." She shone a torch into Sacha's eyes, then made some notes, before pressing her fingers around Sacha's neck. She sat down again and made more notes. I looked sideways and tried to read them, but couldn't decipher the writing.

The doctor held out her hands and asked Sacha to grip them both. "Squeeze hard, please." There was a pause as Sacha seemed to be doing her best, then the doctor said, "OK thanks." She looked at me. "The left is quite a bit weaker."

"What does that mean?" I asked, conscious of a slight tremor in my voice.

"It could be lots of things. Anything or nothing at all..."

I didn't think that was particularly helpful, but kept my thoughts to myself.

"I'd like to refer Sacha to the John Radcliffe paediatric team. They'll do some tests, and we'll know what this is for sure."

"What kind of tests?" I asked.

"They'll want to do a CT scan of her head, to rule out anything we might be missing. Better safe than sorry."

A few days later, Sacha and I were in the John Radcliffe. Once all the forms were signed, she was changed into a hospital gown and asked to lie on a narrow bed in front of what looked like a giant white doughnut. A radiographer came over to me and said, "The nurse here will keep an eye on her." She gestured at a nurse sitting in the corner who gave me a smile that I supposed was meant to be reassuring. "Can you move to the waiting area, please, Mum?

Resisting the temptation to point out to this woman that she was not my daughter, I got up. Sacha lifted her head and gave me a thumbs-up sign. "All good, Mum, I'll be fine."

In the waiting area, I sat on an uncomfortable plastic chair and thumbed through a copy of *Woman's Own*, but none of the pictures or articles registered. The only woman I was interested in was the one having her own head photographed from the inside.

After what seemed like several hours – but I suspect was only one – Sacha came out with the radiographer. She was back in her clothes but looked a little frail. I gave her a hug, then stood back.

"You OK, love?" I asked, and she nodded. "When do we get the results?" I said to the radiographer.

"A couple of days. You'll get a call from your doctor."

In the event, we didn't get a call from her, but from the hospital.

I'd been hovering by the phone ever since we'd got home, reluctant to go out in case it rang (this was long before mobiles, when the only phones we had were fixed to a line in the house). Whenever it did ring, I'd pounce on it before Barry or Sacha could get close, and each time it was not the doctor, I felt both elated and guilty at the same time. Elated, because I had persuaded myself that the longer we didn't hear, the more likely it was because there was nothing to worry about. If it was bad news, my reasoning went, then they would tell us quickly. And I felt guilty, because I couldn't justify my elation when the health of my daughter could still be bad.

So when finally there was a caller who began, "This is the John Radcliffe..." my heart sank.

Not the doctor from the Deddington Health Centre. This must be bad. Numbly I agreed to bring Sacha in to the hospital for a meeting with the paediatric registrar.

He was a kindly looking man, who led me, Barry and Sacha into an anonymous-looking office with some flat backlit screens on the wall.

"Please, sit down." His tone was gentle but serious. "I've reviewed Sacha's scan with the consultant. He'd like to see you."

A few minutes later, a tall man with silver hair came in. The consultant. He probably introduced himself, but I don't remember his name. He shook hands with me and Barry, and nodded kindly to Sacha.

"Right then," he said. "I've had a good look at your scans, Sacha, and I'm afraid we've found something that does cause us some concern."

Concern? My heart started racing.

The registrar slid some black X-ray-type films onto the backlit screens. We all studied them. There was a series of grey and white oval images, with what looked like almost comedic bug-eyes at the front. I glanced at Sacha. Which part of my beautiful daughter's head was I seeing from the inside? I felt a little sick; something so weird couldn't really be her.

The consultant got up and pointed at one of the images.

"You see this area?" His finger indicated the right side. "There's a tumour here, which would explain the problem with your left hand." I struggled to see what he was pointing at; it all looked the same swirly grey and white to me.

"That's the right side," Barry pointed out. "It's her left hand with the funnies." This was the name we'd given to Sacha's strange sensations, as if we could make them seem so trivial that they would fade away.

The consultant shook his head. "The right hemisphere of the brain controls the left hand. This is due to the principle of brain lateralisation, where the left side of the body is generally controlled by the right side of the brain, and vice versa."

I stiffened in my chair. It was on the tip of my tongue to yell, *This is my daughter's head we're talking about! You're telling us she has a tumour – cancer – and you're giving us a fucking biology lesson?* But somehow, I managed to keep my mouth shut.

The consultant's finger moved to another part of the image. "There's also one here. And here. And here."

I could hardly get my breath. It felt as if he'd poured a bucket of iced water over me.

"There's more than one?" I whispered.

"Yes." He gave what I suspect passed for a smile. "But I want you to understand that not all tumours are the same. This appears to be what we call a low-grade astrocytoma. These are slow-growing tumours that arise from cells called astrocytes."

"Is it...?" Barry couldn't finish the question. But we all knew what word he meant.

The big C.

"Is it cancer?" the consultant finished for him. "Technically, yes, but low-grade astrocytomas are quite different from what most people think of as brain cancer. They grow very slowly, sometimes over many years. They don't spread to different parts of the body like other cancers can."

Sacha asked in a flat, almost detached voice, "What does that mean for me?"

"Well, we need to do a few more tests first. We'll need to do what's called a biopsy, where we take a small sample of the tumour tissue, to confirm exactly what type it is. That will help us plan the best treatment."

"Treatment?" I whispered.

"For low-grade astrocytomas in young people like Sacha, we generally watch and wait. Some of these tumours can remain stable for years without causing problems. If it does grow or cause more symptoms, we have options – mainly radiotherapy."

"Or surgery?" This was Barry.

The consultant shook his head. "That's not an option, I'm afraid,
Mr Gregory," he pointed back at the scans. "The tumours are spread all round the brain." He looked up at the corner of the ceiling a moment, as if he was trying to find the right simile. "It's as if you dropped red paint into a pot of white and gave it a good shake. The tumour cells are too mixed in with the normal ones."

He returned to his seat. "I know this is an enormous shock. But many people with low-grade astrocytomas live long lives. We've caught this early, and Sacha is young and healthy otherwise."

"What about school?" Sacha asked. We'd found her a new one, and as I had thought, she was settling in already.

"For now, you can continue as normal. We'll want to see you regularly for check-ups and repeat scans. If your symptoms get worse; more severe headaches, changes in your vision, or increased weakness in your hand, you must contact us immediately." He paused, again seeming to be searching for the right words. "Every case is different," he said carefully. "But many people with low-grade astrocytomas have a good life expectancy. The key is careful monitoring and acting quickly if anything changes."

The registrar stood up. "We'll be in touch for the biopsy," he said, in a way that made it clear that the meeting was now over. I staggered out of my chair, clutching at Barry for support.

A moment later, we were in the car, although I couldn't say how we got there.

Cancer...

My beautiful daughter had cancer...

"You heard what the doctor said," Barry observed as he did up his seatbelt. "Lots of people with this thing live long lives."

Yes, I thought. *But he didn't say how long that actually was.*

Me and Wayne at the Camden Antiques Market

One from the family album from around this time – with me and Wayne manning our stand at the antiques market.

Chapter Twenty-Six

Becoming A Weekend Antique Dealer

The constant worry of Sacha's illness was traumatic and painful enough on its own. Add in that we had only recently moved out of London and needed to establish ourselves in Oxfordshire, and you have the potential recipe for a complete breakdown of family life.

And yet... somehow we managed to keep it all together. I think for the most part this was down to Sacha herself. She had taken two of the silver-haired consultant's comments to heart: one, that the cancer was unlikely to spread; and two, that it was possible to live a long and fulfilling life, despite the swirling mass of tumours in her brain. Based on these, she was determined to live as normally as possible.

"The key thing, Mum," she would often say, "is that this is not terminal. I'm sure I'll live to be an old lady – just one who happens to have had a load of brain tumours since she was a teenager. So I'll just get on with my life."

The hospital did as they said, and saw Sacha regularly for check-ups. All through her A-Levels, then her Equine Management degree at Moreton Merrell College near Stratford-upon-Avon, they monitored the tumours with CT scans and generally professed themselves satisfied that the disease remained stable.

"You see, Mum?" Sacha said to me in the car on the way home after one such scan. "It's not getting any worse. And if it's stayed the same for this many years, what's to say it won't for many more to come?"

I wished I had her confidence, but hers was I so infectious I gave in. I smiled and said, "Of course, darling."

But inevitably there came a time when the results did show some change. The 'funnies' got worse after she graduated, and the hospital decided they needed to start radiotherapy.

Sacha, Barry and I sat in the same room with the same consultant (whose silver hair was now thinner), looking at the same black X-ray-type films on the same backlit screens. Only this time the consultant seemed even more concerned.

"This tumour mass has grown," he said, pointing at a patch on the image. I still couldn't see what he meant – but took him at his word. "And there are more areas affected." He pointed at several more indistinguishable parts of the image.

Sacha leaned forward. "But it's still only in my head?" she asked, her voice unnaturally calm. "It's not spreading anywhere else?"

"We don't think so," he replied. "Your lymph glands are clear, and the scans are not showing any metastases."

"That's OK, then," Sacha said, sitting back. I also let out the breath I'd been holding.

"But we need to be sure," he said. "We want to start radiotherapy."

My chest tightened. "Will that make her sick?" I asked. I knew chemotherapy had that effect, but didn't know about radiotherapy.

"It's possible it might make the symptoms worse initially," he replied. "It can cause the brain to swell and may result in tiredness and sickness. But this should only be temporary." He frowned, as if choosing the right words. "But there is one other side effect that might happen."

"Which is?" Barry asked.

"We'll be using something known as 'whole brain radiotherapy', and it is not unknown for there to be substantive hair loss across the entire scalp."

"I'll lose my hair?" Sacha whispered.

"Almost certainly. But it should start to grow back in a few months after we finish the course of therapy."

"And that will be that?" Sacha asked. "I can get on with life?"

"I do hope so," he said.

So we fitted her radiotherapy treatment around our busy lives. Despite being sick more frequently and occasionally losing the use of her left hand for a time, Sacha was still convinced the disease was manageable, and she would grow old with it. "It's just the radiotherapy," she declared. "The doctor said it would make things worse before it gets better."

Even when her beautiful hair started coming out in clumps, she remained upbeat. "He said we should expect this," she observed. "It'll grow back."

I looked at the hairbrush she held, clogged with a mass of blonde locks. "If you are sure it will regrow..."

"Of course. Come on Mum, smile! We'll get through this."

Such positivity was infectious, and there were times when I let it carry me along. I found myself laughing and chatting with her on the long round trips to and from the John Radcliffe. And when the chat stopped, we would enjoy companionable silences instead. We even had fun picking out wigs, with us both in fits of laughter as she tried on ever more weird and wonderful hairstyles.

But through it all something didn't change. She was still my beautiful daughter. My companion. My friend.

We would watch the TV together in the evenings; me sitting with my shoes off and my feet tucked up under me, Barry in his chair with his attention more on his newspaper, while Sacha would be stretched out on the sofa in her pyjamas. The light would bounce off her gleaming head, now fully bald apart from a few determined tufts clinging resolutely to her scalp.

One evening I found myself giving her a sidelong glance, trying to reconcile this strange-looking person with the daughter I had raised. She still had the same warm, kindly eyes – just not currently looking out from under a blonde fringe. Her mouth and nose hadn't changed – they were still beautifully proportioned and extremely pretty. But there was no escaping the truth of the situation; she had a head full of tumours, and however strong she was being, however much radiotherapy she had, they didn't seem to be going away.

And yet... How could I justify fearing the worst all the time, when she was seeing only the best?

So I had to be positive as well. What choice did I have?

And on that basis, life went on.

The cottage we bought in Deddington had come with a large barn, which had been one of the things that first sold us on the property. It was at the original viewing, while I was in the kitchen chatting with the agent, that I realised Barry was no longer with us. He must have wandered off somewhere.

We eventually found him standing in the barn, looking around with one of his 'I've got a great idea' expressions.

"What are you thinking, Barry?" I enquired.

He gave me a slow grin. "Antiques shop," he said, with the flourish of a magician producing a rabbit from the hat. "There's good road access and parking, and this space is big, light and airy." He pointed up at the roof. "And it looks like it's watertight; no mould or musty smell." He waved his hand round the large space, which currently contained a few hay bales, some broken garden machinery, and what looked suspiciously like an old feeding trough. "It's perfect. Clear out all this crap and we have the ideal shop." He waved at the far corner. "Large pieces over there, art in the other corner. Bric-a-brac in some display cabinets as you come in. There's even space for your antique textiles and clothing." His grin was infectious. "And this part of Oxfordshire is great for antiques – people round here buy tons of it for their big old houses."

"What about stock?" I asked. "We'll still need to buy." Another thought came to me. "And you've got a lot of regular customers in London. They won't come out all the way here."

"True..." he said, then brightened. "We can still commute to the market in Hampstead at the weekends." His grin broadened. "We can sell here in Deddington in the week, and at the weekends, we can buy and sell in London."

Which is what we ended up doing. In the week, we sold out of the barn, with Sacha helping. She discovered she had a real talent for 'Front of House' work, and would approach potential customers who wandered in, apparently looking only to browse. She would soon have them buying an item, even if it was something small, like an old piece of Wedgewood, a teddy bear, or maybe a tin garage sign. If they were looking for furniture or a painting, she directed them to Barry, and if their interest was more into textiles and clothing, she sent them my way.

At the weekends, we closed the shop, loaded the van with any stock that we thought was more likely to sell in London, and drove down. Initially we would go the night before, so we would be ready for a very early start on the Saturday morning. This meant taking up an invitation from our old neighbours, Tony and Helga, to stay with them in Goldhurst Terrace.

The first time we turned into the terrace, I shivered, as if someone had 'walked over my grave'.

"What is it?" Barry asked.

"It just seems weird," I said, as he drove slowly along the road, looking for a parking spot. "We're in Goldhurst Terrace, but we can't just walk up to our own front door and go in."

He glanced at me. "Does that really bother you? I thought you were desperate to move to the country."

"I was," I said. "It's just... weird. That's all."

He gave a small chuckle. "Have a glass of wine with Tony and Helga, and it'll all seem better."

"Maybe just the one."

His chuckle became a full laugh. "You'll be lucky. They drink like a pair of fish, those two."

He parked the van, and we knocked on their door. "Annabelle! Barry!" Tony exclaimed with a broad grin when he saw us. After the obligatory hug for me and a shake of Barry's hand, he ushered us in.

Helga already had the table laid, and to confirm Barry's worst suspicions, there were four bottles of wine at one end. Tony ushered us to our seats and poured us a large glass each.

"So, tell us all about Oxfordshire..." he began.

Three hours later, I collapsed fully dressed onto the bed, aware that the room was already spinning like a fairground ride. I was rocked almost over the edge as Barry fell onto his side of the bed. He gave a loud belch. "That last whish..." he tried. "That lasht whishky... was one too many..." There was another belch, followed almost immediately by an even louder snore. The first of many.

At 4 a.m., the alarm went off, and I struggled awake, dry-mouthed and with a splitting headache. I rolled over and thumped Barry.

"Wake up," I muttered. "Gotta get going!"

There was a groan from the other side of the bed, but after a few minutes, we were both up.

"Oh Christ," Barry said, looking blearily at me. "We're both still dressed."

We stayed with Tony and Helga a few more times, until we decided our livers could no longer cope. We'd tried protesting, putting our hands over our glasses when he went to pour top-ups, citing our early start – all to no avail. Tony would not accept anything other than total alcoholic compliance, as if he was on a personal mission to get us as drunk as possible every weekend.

After one particularly excessive booze-filled evening, I said to Barry as we drove away the following morning, "We could always get up a couple of hours earlier at home, and drive straight to the market?"

"Good idea," he muttered. "Very good idea."

'Nettles in a blue and white jug'

Collage. 29cm x 28cm.

Coming across this collage brought a lump to my throat – it reminded me of a time when Sacha and I painted the floor of my workroom in the Deddington Cottage. A lovely moment of togetherness and fun.

Chapter Twenty-Seven

Becoming A Life Class Teacher

In my determination to make our lives as normal as possible, I wanted to keep up with my art. The urge to be creative with paints, pens and collage still burned strong, despite the family situation. It was almost as if my brain was fighting for some form of normality, while Sacha's was fighting against the tumours. So I sought opportunities whenever I could to set up my easel, whether it was painting nature outside or collaging in the back room at the cottage.

I also looked for life classes, but there were none locally. I didn't want to travel too far afield in case Sacha needed me, either for a hospital appointment, or if her 'funnies' were too bad.

"If there are no life classes in the immediate area, why don't you start your own, Mum?" Sacha asked one day. We were sitting together in the kitchen, both cupping our hands round mugs of tea. "The back room is plenty big enough, and you can get models to come in and sit for you." She pushed back a lock of auburn hair that was in danger of falling into the tea, (her wig was auburn this week, last week it had been brunette). "There's a woman at work who told me she's done some sitting." Sacha had now got a job at a local feed and farm supplies merchant, after doing a secretarial course in Oxford. "Her name is Maria, and she says she's looking for a bit of extra income."

Maria turned out to be a trim no-nonsense, middle-aged woman, and she readily agreed to sit if I could get a class together. So I started putting the word out, and fairly soon I started receiving enquiries.

"You see, Mum?" Sacha said triumphantly when I showed her the list of names, "you've uncovered an unmet need for local people who are just busting to draw a naked body."

I decided to limit the class to fifteen places, and we soon had it established: two hours every Thursday afternoon, with Maria sitting as the model and me helping the class to improve their skills.

It seemed strange, after years of studying under Jack Yates in Camden, that here I was, being the teacher myself. But I found myself increasing in confidence, offering advice that seemed well-received, and the standard of work produced by the class seemed to get steadily better.

The life classes were becoming established, but they were not my full-time business. This was the trade in antique textiles and clothing I had originally started back in London. While I put a few notable pieces out in the barn to attract the buyers, the real work was done from an upstairs bedroom that had originally been earmarked for Wayne. But since he had moved into his own flat in the village, I'd taken it over. Regular customers, or people interested in a vintage garment, were invited up to the room so they could browse at their leisure and try clothes on.

Sacha wandered in one afternoon, as I was sorting through a pile of linens. The lower-value items were going in a black bin bag, while the more expensive pieces were being carefully packed into a suitcase.

"You going somewhere, Mum?" she enquired, taking a pile of clothes I hadn't yet classified off the visitor's chair. This was a Regency dining chair in mahogany with a gently curved back rail, brass-studded leather upholstery and turned legs. I'd 'borrowed' it from one of Barry's house-clearances, looking for something that matched the aesthetic of my antique textiles. "It's a great example of English craftsmanship at its finest," he'd said as he helped me carry it up the stairs.

"I just think it's beautiful," I'd commented, standing back to admire it once we'd positioned it in the corner. "Just what I want."

Sacha sat down on it, stretched her legs out, then tucked them under her, grinning like the cat who had discovered the perfect spot and had no intention of moving for hours. She pointed at the suitcase. "Where are you off to?"

"Nowhere," I said, closing it up. "But I'm clearing the room so I can paint the floor."

She looked down and shrugged. "Why? They're nice boards. Do they need painting?"

"Yes," I replied. "They're boring. The floor needs 'zhuzhing' up."

"OK. Do you want a hand?"

Together we masked out the floor ready for the design I had envisaged; a series of blue and white alternating squares, as if it was tiled. Crawling backwards from the furthest corner towards the door, we painted first the white, then, when that was dry, the blue. It took us a whole day, and involved frequent stops for tea and biscuits, as well as plenty of laughter. My technique was to work round the outside of the square first then fill in, while Sacha's was to pour a pool of paint into the middle, before working it out to the edges. This involved a surprising level of accuracy in the amount of paint she poured, as well as a level of abandon as she slapped it outwards with her brush.

"You've got quite a lot of paint in your hair," I pointed out, after a blue tile had been finished in a particularly vigorous way.

"Oh blow," she said, taking her wig off and examining it. "I'll clean it later." She threw it out of the door, where it sat like a small brown puppy waiting for its mistress. "That's better," she said, scratching her head. "It was getting itchy anyway."

"Now you've got paint on your head," I observed.

"What, here?" She dabbed a brushful on her temple.

"No, here," I said, painting a line from her forehead to the back of her neck.

"Oh, I thought you meant here." She added more paint above her other ear.

I observed her critically. "Now it's all uneven," I squinted across my upturned brush. "It needs a bit here. And here." I stood back. "That's better. Lovely. I think I'll exhibit you in the Tate."

There was the scuff of a shoe in the doorway. "Is this a women-only head-painting session?" Barry asked. "Or can anyone join in?"

※

Fast forward a few years to the late 1980s, when Margaret Thatcher's government raised interest rates to around fifteen per cent. Sadly this put us in an unfortunate position with our overall borrowing.

Barry sat me and Sacha down in the kitchen and gave us the bad news.

"We're too stretched," he said simply. "We've got the mortgage on the cottage, as well as the shop in town, and the rent on the room where you do your life classes." The shop was a store called Tuckers that we'd taken over when it came up for sale a year or two before. We'd cleared the barn and set up a more formal selling space for the antiques on the ground floor at Tuckers, while my textiles were on the top floor. The barn had become a space for entertaining, and we'd held some pretty wild parties in there, with me, Sacha and Barry dancing the night away with the many friends we'd made in Deddington and the surrounding towns. Ingrid came over as well, and so did my mother, who now ran a dress shop in Banbury.

Meanwhile, the life classes had got too big for the space they'd been in – a corner of the textiles room above the shop. It had been such a bother to move the stock every week to make space, so I'd found a room to rent in the old Town Hall, a landmark building standing on its own in the Market Place. It was fascinating; a strange-looking house appearing to be supported in the air by a series of brick arches.

"We're going to need to sell up," Barry continued. As Sacha and I looked open-mouthed at him, he added, "I'm sorry, but I've looked at it every which way, and we really don't have any other option."

"The textiles are doing really well," I said. I'd even bought myself a new(ish) car with the profits; a particularly nippy little red Nissan Micra. "Can't we ride this out?"

"I don't see how," Barry replied with a shake of his head. "Even with the money I'm bringing in, we can never afford the new payments."

"But I'm earning," Sacha pointed out. "Maybe I can contribute more?"

Barry put his hand over hers. "That's good of you, Sacha love," he said softly. "But it's still a drop in the ocean." He shook his head. "And anyway, you need to concentrate on keeping yourself well, not worrying about money. You don't want to have to go through all that radiotherapy again. Especially now your hair's grown back."

It was settled. The shop went to a restaurateur called Jamie Dexter and we put the cottage up for sale. In the end, it was sold for less than we wanted, as the high interest rates had depressed the market. Although as Barry pointed out, we were lucky to have sold it at all.

We found a rental property called Orchard House a couple of miles away in the village of Barford St Michael. After our lovely cottage, Orchard House was something of a come down. Everything stank of the previous occupant's smoke, which had made the curtains so brown they had to be thrown away immediately.

But we made it pleasant enough. It had a lovely dining room, and once we had the house looking as good as we could make it, we started holding regular dinner parties. My mother was often invited, and although she was getting quite frail, she did come over a few times.

"Good heavens, Annabelle," she said when she came through the front door one evening. "What on earth are you wearing?"

As I recall, I had dressed in the fashion of the time; a cream pleated skirt, over-sized pink blazer with brass buttons and large shoulder pads (Alexis Colby had nothing on me), nude tights and chunky heels. The late 1980s was a time when I enjoyed the fashions. I felt they suited my figure, and for a lady nearing fifty, they made me feel quite stylish and elegant.

"I think Mummy looks great, Grandma," Sacha chipped in from behind me, ever my wing-woman.

"I think it looks too... American," Mother said, her perfectly plucked eyebrow raised. "Quite unacceptable." On that friendly note, she tottered past me towards the dining room, pausing only briefly when she got to Sacha. "How are you feeling, sweetie?" she asked. "Still getting headaches?"

"Yes, Grandma. But they've been the same for years now. No worse."

"Good." There was a pause, and I could feel them both looking at my back. "Now for goodness sake, Sacha," Mother said in an appallingly loud stage-whisper, "can you not get your mother to dress properly?"

There was a silence, then the sound of heels clacking away down the passage.

"Really, Mummy," Sacha came up and whispered in my ear, "I do think you can try harder. What were you thinking?" Then she snorted with laughter. "Was she always like that?"

"Oh yes." My stomach knotted with hurt as the vision came to me of the fairy dress hanging out of reach on the wall. Then the hurt became anger. I was sixteen again and had just got myself into St Martin's. Instead of congratulations, all my mother had given me was criticism of my sweater dress, beret and yellow ballet flats, standing before me with her hands on her hips, gasping, "You just turned up like... that?"

"Oh yes," I repeated to Sacha. "Always."

For a woman who had raised three daughters in such poverty she couldn't even afford to have the whole family live in the same dwelling at the same time, Mother had turned into an unconscionable snob. I blamed Dior; before her role as a 'Madame' in the salon in Conduit Street, she'd been a lot more down-to-earth.

Dinner that evening was somewhat strained, with Mother frequently glancing across at my blazer and wincing visibly. I half expected her to whip out a pair of sunglasses from her over-sized Gucci bag, as if to shield her eyes from my outfit.

At least she kept quiet over the pudding, a greengage and plum crumble.

"These are your own fruits from the garden?" she asked Sacha, still avoiding looking at me.

"They are, Grandma."

"Very good. They should be prized. Tell your mother to make sure they get plenty of water."

"You can tell her yourself, Grandma," Sacha observed. "She's right in front of you."

Mother shook her head. "I can't see past the garish jacket," she said. "And certainly not beyond the glare of those awful buttons."

Sacha's health had, as she told her grandmother, remained fairly stable post-radiotherapy, and she continued to maintain her positive outlook. She even decided to get two kittens, and became obsessed with these bundles of fluff, naming them after the two kids in *The Flintstones*. Pebbles was a good-natured and even-tempered little girl, whereas her brother Bamm-Bamm was full of mischief, and always finding trouble.

Orchard Cottage was opposite a small lane, at the end of which was a stone barn with a pitched roof and church-style window. This was Woodworm Studios; the recording facility set up by Dave Pegg of Fairport Convention. Bamm-Bamm found it an irresistible playground; he would head over the road and saunter in whenever he felt like it, no doubt because he enjoyed the attention from the musicians who recorded there, such as Fairport Convention themselves, as well as bands like Jethro Tull.

One night Barry and I had just retired to bed, and were reading our books, when there was a sudden and insistent knock at the bedroom door. Sacha poked her head in, her eyes wide and her cheeks pale.

"What is it, love?" I asked, fearing that something had happened with her health.

"It's Bamm-Bamm," she whispered. "He's disappeared."

I let out a breath of relief. "Is that all?" I replied, maybe a little too casually. "I'm sure he's around somewhere. You know how easily he gets into tiny spaces."

"But he's never missed his supper before," she insisted.

"That is bad," Barry observed. He was never one to miss his supper either – so presumably he felt strong affinity for Bamm-Bamm's predicament.

"We'll help you find him," I said, swinging my legs out of bed and shuffling into my slippers.

We walked around the house calling his name, peering into all the nooks and crannies that an enterprising young cat could sneak into. But there was no little 'meow' from a dark corner, nor a pair of bright green eyes staring back at us in the torchlight.

"I really don't know where he is," Sacha wailed, and I could see how distressed she was becoming. "Maybe he's dead!"

"Let's try the garden," Barry suggested. "He's bound to be out there somewhere."

Orchard House had a large garden, so large that Barry had had to get a sit-on lawnmower. We searched under every bush and pointed our torches up at every tree – and there were a fair few of those – but again, no sign of Bamm-Bamm. At one point Barry suddenly shushed us both, saying, "I think I heard something." Sacha and I stopped talking, and we all stood still, our ears pricked for the slightest feline sound. But there was nothing more than the wind rustling through the trees, then the distant hoot of an owl. "Ah, sorry. Must have been that," said Barry. "Carry on."

Our search remained fruitless (or should that be 'catless'?), for another hour. Sacha's distress was becoming ever more worrying, and she was continually sniffling, and saying things like, "He's dead. I know it. A fox has him. Poor little Bamm-Bamm..."

Eventually, it was clear we had searched and called as much as we could, and it was a disconsolate Gregory threesome who made their way indoors and hung their anoraks back on the hooks.

"Where can he possibly have got to_?" Sacha began, then stopped, as the blare of a burglar alarm suddenly ripped through the night. We looked at each other in shock; the noise was coming from the Woodworm Studios.

What could possibly have set off a motion sensor alarm in a recording studio?

The three of us came to the same realisation at the same time. Of course it might have been a burglar, but perhaps it was...

"Bamm-Bamm!" we all said together.

We rushed out of the house and across the road, just in time to see Dave Pegg coming out of the studio holding a small bundle of furry mischief by the neck.

"Yours, I believe?" he muttered, thrusting Bamm-Bamm into Sacha's welcoming arms. Then he spun round and stomped back into the studio without another word.

'Pippin Apples'

Collage. 20cm x 22cm.

I don't recall when I did this collage of apples in a pot, but it might well have been as a result of finding the 'Modbury Pippin' restaurant in Devon.

Chapter Twenty-Eight

Becoming At Home In Devon

A year after we had moved into Orchard House, Barry sat me and Sacha down in the kitchen – and from the look on his face, it felt as if we were once again going to get some bad news.

"I've had a letter from the landlord," he began, holding up a piece of paper.

This sounded ominous; Sacha and I exchanged worried glances.

We were not wrong.

"We have a month to vacate," Barry continued, his face creased into a worried frown.

Sacha gave a small squeak of concern; she'd still been getting her 'funnies', and any change – such as a stressful and rushed move – would be very disruptive for her health.

"Why?" I asked. "Don't they know about Sacha?"

Barry waved the letter at us. "That doesn't seem to bother them."

"But we've settled in!" I said, as if that alone was enough of a reason. "We've got the place looking the way we want it. Looking beautiful."

"I'm sorry, Annabelle love, but they say the decision is made." He gave us a weak smile. "I've checked with the agent, and he confirms it."

"Oh." I gave this some thought. We'd need to find somewhere else as quick as possible – which meant we'd probably have little choice. We'd most likely end up with somewhere perfectly ghastly.

"There is some good news," Barry said, breaking into my thoughts. "I've been doing some sums, and I think this time we can buy instead of renting." He smiled. "At least we won't be chucked out again."

I was right about the limited choices we'd have. The place we found for a quick purchase was in Adderbury, a village about five miles from Orchard House. Croft Cottage itself was a lovely old building, with eight big arched windows, a central front door and a gently pitched roof with chimneys at either end. Inside, there was a wide staircase over three floors, two bathrooms and a big office Barry and I could share. Sacha was delighted; she had a bedroom with a shower room on a landing that was exclusively hers.

The downside – and it was indeed a ghastly one – was that Croft Cottage was on the main A4260 Oxford Road, with only a narrow pavement between our front door and the heavy traffic thundering past on its way into the town. The volume – both in number and noise – of cars, lorries and buses was appalling. There was rarely a time when the whole house was not shaking as a twenty-tonne lorry roared past.

Sacha did everything she could to make sure Bamm-Bamm stayed away from the front door. She was quite rightly worried that if he slipped out and tried to cross the road, he wouldn't have stood a chance. She did, however, allow him out into the back garden. This was as calm and peaceful as the front was noisy. It was a secluded space surrounded by high brick walls with climbing roses, clematis and wisteria. Lavender and geraniums were in the beds, and I later added some dahlias and alliums for even more vibrant colour. The middle of the garden was full of beautiful damson trees, which were laden in season with deep purple fruit.

Unsurprisingly, my mother was not impressed with the traffic at the front, but she made all the right noises when we showed her the garden at the back. "Damsons!" she exclaimed, and had Barry bring her a stepladder so she could get up high enough to pick the plum-like fruit. She then made Sacha stand at the foot of the ladder with a basket, ready to catch the pickings as she dropped them down. Poor Sacha had to run around like a Wimbledon ball-girl as the fruit came at her from all directions.

The end did seem to justify the means, though, as the damson jam Mother made was delicious, and it soon became a staple on our breakfast toast.

We were in the Croft Cottage for nearly four years, but I never really warmed to it. For me the ugliness of the A4260 overshadowed the building and the garden, and I was always alive to the possibility of moving again.

The key factor was Sacha. She was still working at the feed merchants, driving herself there most days, but if the 'funnies' were bad, I would drive her in the morning and pick her up at the end of the day. While the funnies didn't dent her confidence that she could keep going and carry on for the rest of her life, I was never so sure. My concern was the ongoing noise and pollution from the road, and how this might affect her.

I spoke to Barry about it one afternoon, while Sacha was at work.

"She needs a more peaceful, calm environment," I said. "I can't imagine that continually breathing all those fumes is not going to have an effect."

"We have to do all we can for her," Barry agreed. "What do you suggest?"

"Somewhere nearby," I said. "What with my art taking off locally." A few of my pieces had recently been accepted into an exhibition by the Oxford Arts Society at the Museum of Modern Art in Oxford. Exhibiting at least six works was a prerequisite for getting into the Society of Women Artists – a prestigious national organisation that only accepted new members when one of the existing ones resigned or died. I was an Associate Member and had managed to get my name near the top of the list for full membership.

Barry shrugged. "I don't think it needs to be local for that. I have been thinking about Devon, and there's a thriving art scene in the South West, too."

"Devon?" I replied. "Why there particularly?"

"You remember I went down there a few weeks ago on business?" I nodded. "I was in a town called Ashburton, on the edge of Dartmoor." His eyes shone. "You'd love it, Annabelle. It's peaceful and rural, but there are cities like Exeter and Plymouth if you need anything. I'm going back down in a few days. Why don't you come too and have a scout around? See if you like it."

Barry was right – Ashburton was picture perfect; everything I could have wished for. But it was not just the one town; I felt completely at home in Devon itself. It had a natural beauty to it: the broad sweep of the moors, the golden sandy beaches, the picture postcard villages with their tiny streets and old-world appeal. Even the narrow country roads with their high hedges on both sides that had few, if any, passing places seemed to have a charm all of their own, and I couldn't help but chuckle at Barry's mutterings as he had to back up for hundreds of yards each time it was our turn to give way to oncoming cars.

As we drove though the county with the fields and trees and hedges wafting past, I found myself relaxing more and more. This was where we could live in peace. Where Sacha could maintain her strength and quality of life. Where I could paint. Where I had space to think. Where I could be at one with nature and walk under a wide-open sky.

In that moment of realisation, I was no longer a woman in her fifties. I was once again the little girl on stage in her dreadful old rabbit costume, vowing to seek out beauty in her life.

Was this where my journey would come to an end? Had I finally found what I had been seeking?

Barry brought me back to the present.

"Maybe we can find a good place to run the antiques business," he suggested, as we drove through the narrow lanes.

"Yes," I agreed.

We concentrated on looking for a suitable empty shop, checking in each town and village, and asking in commercial estate agents. But we continually got the same answer, "Sorry, nothing at the moment."

By the time we drove down the steep hill into the little town of Modbury, we were in despair. Barry was talking seriously about giving up and staying in Adderbury, while I was slumped in my seat, seeing the dream I had just begun to hope for starting to fade away.

We found a space in a car park just off Church Street and walked back to the shops. I spotted a little restaurant called the Modbury Pippin that had an 'open' sign hanging crookedly in the door.

"My mouth is dry," I said. "I could do with a cup of tea."

Inside was dark and very drab, and all the tables were completely empty. A clock ticked in the dusty silence. We stood a moment, unsure if we should leave, when an old lady shuffled in. "Can I help you, my lovers?" she asked.

"Um... Tea for two?" I enquired.

"Surely, surely. Take a seat." She shuffled out again.

Trying not to laugh, Barry and I sat down and waited. The room was bigger than I would have expected from the outside, and I could see there were further rooms off this one. "It's actually quite extensive," I whispered.

"Yes," he whispered back.

There was a short silence, then I asked, "Why are we whispering?"

"You started it."

"Seemed natural."

"Hardly."

There was a creak from the doorway and the rattle of crockery on a tray.

"Shh," I breathed.

"Here you are, my lovers." She put the tray down and took off the cups and teapot. "Not seen you here before," she observed, standing by the table with the look of someone who was not only desperate to talk, but also very interested in everyone else's business.

"We're from Oxford," I told her. "Only down for a few days."

"We're thinking of bringing our antiques business here to Devon," Barry added. "But there don't seem to be any suitable shop premises available."

"Oh." She appeared to be looking for the right words. "Well... I'm putting this one up for sale. The board goes up tomorrow."

There was another silence, as Barry and I exchanged glances. *This could be ideal* was the thought on both our minds.

"But there's not much need for antiques in Modbury," she continued. "The tourists want feeding, not furniture." She poured the teas. "I know it's quiet now, but at the height of the season we're always busy." She stood back, still holding the teapot. "There's much more call for hospitality in the town. If you know anything about catering, then this place would be ideal for you." She put the pot down. "And there's plenty of accommodation upstairs. Enough for a family if you have children. This is a business where you could live above the premises."

Barry and I gave each other another look. *We could live and work here. But... could we really give up the antiques? Get back into hospitality?*

"That does sound interesting," Barry said, then he paused. "How much are you asking?"

The Altar used as a Bar in Bistro 35

It is now in my conservatory, as I could never
let it go after I closed the Bistro.
Too many memories are tied up in this beautiful piece.

Chapter Twenty-Nine

Becoming the Heart And Soul

Her name was Mrs Mullery, and she was the sole owner of the Modbury Pippin at 35 Church Street. We put Croft Cottage on the market, and were able to make a reasonably quick sale, with the purchase in Modbury going through shortly after. It was relatively trouble-free as Mrs Mullery was keen to sell up and retire.

During the negotiations, we had come to the conclusion there was no way we could move in immediately; there was so much work needed, both to the public rooms downstairs, and to the private ones above. So when we moved from Oxfordshire, we transferred to a rental cottage in the little coastal village of Hope Cove, around eleven miles from Modbury.

One warm summer's evening, Sacha and I sat together on the beach at Mouthwell Sands, our arms round each other and our hair whipping across each other's faces. The rich red and orange sky merged into the sea on the horizon, the waves crashing as they reached up the sandy beach, then hissing as they were sucked back into the sea.

I pointed over to our left, across the headland at Bolt Tail. "Alderney," I said. "Somewhere over that way."

Sacha snuggled into my shoulder as she followed my finger. "We had fun there didn't we, Mum?"

"Mm," I agreed. I looked at her profile, lit with a golden hue from the setting sun. "Once we've got the new place set up, we can go back to Alderney for a holiday if you want."

Her head came round, and her lovely blue eyes held mine. There was a sadness there I hadn't seen before. "What is it, Sacha love?" I asked.

"Oh Mum, there won't be any more holidays."

"What do you mean?"

She shook her head, and the corners of her mouth turned down. "The truth is... I don't think I've got much longer."

"Don't be silly, Sacha," I replied, "of course you..." then I faltered to a stop. It had been so many years since that first time in the silver-haired consultant's office and, apart from the time she'd had radiotherapy, she'd been stable enough. I'd been convinced to go along with her certainty she could live a long life despite the tumours. Her regular check-ups had even helped, showing that the cancer hadn't spread. I'd been so concerned to make sure she was never too stressed, because I believed she would be fine if we kept her away from the pressures of life. Of course there had been the funnies, but these had stayed regular and were not happening too often. Unless...

"Is there something you're not telling me, Sacha? Are the funnies getting worse?"

Her eyes widened, and she nodded.

"Oh God, Sacha! Why didn't you let me know?"

"I didn't want to bother you. You and Dad have got so much on at the moment."

I looked back at the sunset, not sure I could form the words to say what was in my mind. *Of course I would want you to tell me. Nothing – nothing – is more important to me than your health. Than having you with me. My daughter. My companion. My friend.*

I found my voice. "Then we need to get you to the hospital," I said. "They need to do a scan, or a CT, or blood tests, or whatever it is they do..."

"If you want, Mum," she said slowly. "But somehow, I know it's not going to help. I'm getting so tired now.

Sometimes I can't get out of bed in the morning. It's as if I can't move when I wake up. As if I'm paralysed." She put her head back on my shoulder. "It's been getting worse over the last few months." Her voice was strangely flat, as if she was merely commenting on the weather. "If it carries on like this, there's only one way it's going. Only one thing that's going to happen."

"No!"

"Yes, Mum." She lifted her head and gave me a deep look. "We have to get used to it. We have to make the best of the time we have left."

There was a long silence as I struggled to come to terms with what she was telling me. My Sacha – my resourceful, funny, loving, beautiful Sacha – couldn't be preparing for her own end. A hot flush of anger gripped me. *I wouldn't allow it! I would find a way to keep her alive, just as she had always assured me!*

As if she'd read my thoughts, Sacha gripped my arm. "No Mum. Let's not fight this. Let's enjoy ourselves for as long as we can." She pulled a lock of her hair off my face. "Let's talk about the future. What are you and Dad going to do with the tea room?"

I could hardly believe what I was hearing. How could she be thinking of that after what she'd just told me? But a quick glance told me she was serious. Taking a long breath, I said, "We're not sure. We're still thinking of a possible antiques shop, or maybe a restaurant."

"Oh not antiques, please!"

"Why not?"

"Boring. I want you and Dad to have fun! Have parties like we used to do in the barn. Be the life and soul. I want you both to enjoy your lives." She looked out to sea a moment, then turned to me. "What's the address again?"

"35 Church Street."

She gave me a triumphant grin. "There it is. Make it a *bistro*! The beating heart and soul of Modbury!" She laughed. "Call it Bistro 35!"

Bistro 35 took shape over the next few weeks, along with our own home on the floor above. I went through the planning and decorating work in a state of numbness; my thoughts directing themselves to the tasks in hand as if they were being done by someone else, while all the time there was really only one thing on my mind – Sacha's well-being.

She would often stay in her bed at Hope Cove for the whole morning, only appearing at lunchtime. Barry or I would stay in the house, doing paperwork or – in my case, painting or collaging – so we could be there if she needed us. While she was obviously slowing down, she would occasionally have enough energy to come with us and help out at the Bistro. Barry and I would make sure she wasn't strained or stressed, as she clearly got much pleasure from seeing the work progress and giving us her opinions.

"This is going to be such a lovely place, Mum," she said one afternoon as we finished painting a wall. "A place of laughter and enjoyment. You and Dad have had such busy lives. This is your chance to relax together and have fun."

I put my brush down and held her face in both hands. "But I want you to enjoy it with us, Sacha love," I whispered. "It won't be the same if you're not here."

She put her own hands over mine and smiled. "I know, Mum, but..." Her eyes flicked over to the wall she'd just painted. "I will always be here, where I've done the painting. Or where I chose a lampshade. Or decided where a chair should go. That is where you'll find me."

Sacha's influence was kept to the Bistro downstairs; the upstairs accommodation was much too unhealthy before we restored it. There was a carpet in the bathroom that looked as if it was incubating the bubonic plague, and when we took up the shower tray, there were solid clumps of newspapers that must have been turned to papier-mâché by the years of damp. Not only did these stink of mould, but they were also peppered with ossified mice droppings.

But we gradually got the work done, and the place became both habitable – and as far as Sacha was concerned, hygienic. Downstairs, the Bistro decoration was finished, and I turned my attention to the pictures we would put on the walls.

"You've got hundreds of pieces of art, Mum," Sacha observed. "Here's your chance to put them up for everyone to see and enjoy."

We agreed there would be some spaces where the pictures would be a permanent fixture, and some where we would regularly rotate them, as if it were an exhibition gallery.

"Where are you putting those?" Barry asked one day, as I laid a stack of my framed nude life drawings against the wall of the room we had decided was going to be the bar. There were even some new ones, done in a class I'd found in Modbury.

"I thought in here," I replied.

He shook his head with a grin. "No, you've got other pieces that can go in here. I think those belong in the loos, and you should change them regularly, so there's always new ones to see."

So the toilets were decorated with my life drawings – which was quite a talking point for the regulars and tourists alike and even prompted a few comments on review sites as well. Although, as I noted earlier, not always complimentary ones.

After hanging the pictures I found Barry back in the same place. He was standing with his hands on his hips. "We need a bar, Annabelle."

"I know. We could get that carpenter chap who did the kitchen upstairs to make one," I suggested. "Unless you want to get some old pianos, like the Lords Club?"

"No, I've got a better idea. There's something in Paignton that might be just the thing. Come on, get in the van and we can go and have a look."

We told Sacha we were going out, and she agreed to wait for us to return. In the van on the way to Paignton, Barry explained his idea. "I've been keeping an eye out for something distinctive and think I might have found it. The Paignton Marist School had an old altar and some pews and they're selling them off. The altar is a real talking-point piece, attributed to William Burges. I thought we could use them all in the bar."

"Won't pews be uncomfortable?" I queried, squirming at the memory of sitting on hard ones as a girl at St James the Less primary school. "We want people to relax and stay a while, not have one drink and rush off with a sore bum."

"Fair point."

We arrived at the sale and soon found the altar in a corner of the showroom.

As Barry had said, it was certainly a talking point. Once we'd moved a couple of chairs out of the way we could appreciate it in all its glory. I immediately saw why he thought it would be such a great piece for the bistro.

"Victorian gothic revival?" I asked.

He nodded, then glanced down at the details in the auction brochure. "Crafted from English oak, the piece features classic Gothic proportions with alternating black and red motifs in the upper section." He gave me a grin then carried on reading. "The front panels showcase extraordinary medieval-inspired inlay work, while a central geometric medallion executed in contrasting woods creates a mandala-like composition. The adjacent panels each depict a medieval angelic figure in illuminated manuscript style, complete with rich blues and golds within a Gothic quatrefoil frame."

"Quatrefoil?"

He tapped the brochure. "That's what it says here." He pointed at the four-leafed clover shape round each of the kneeling 'angel' figures, set against a diamond design. "Quatrefoil." He cleared his throat and went back to the brochure. "Spiralling columns flank the structure on each side, their carved surfaces playing dramatically with the light and shadow." He looked up.

"Beautiful," I breathed. "It will look magnificent in the Bistro." I paused, then asked casually, "But will it fit in the van?"

In the event it did, but only by having it sticking out by a couple of feet, and having the doors tied across it.

Once Barry had settled the payment and put the pews back into the sale, we were ready to leave. As he pulled carefully out of the car park, the van gave a stutter and misfired. He revved the engine, and it caught again. "It's been doing that a bit lately," he muttered. "But it does always seem to keep going."

Sadly, this was the time it decided to break the habit. Which is how I came to be sitting alone in the broken-down van on the side of the Plymouth Road, about a mile outside the village of Follaton. Unable to get a signal on his phone, Barry had tramped back to the village to see if he could find a tow-truck. This left me as the sole guardian of a Victorian altar, complete with Gothic quatrefoil frames.

As the traffic whizzed past, I turned and looked at the heavy piece of Victoriana behind me.

It was going to make a great bar – the kind of quirky, unexpected, but beautiful thing that would make a visit to Bistro 35 a memorable event. Like the pianos in the Lords Club and the clown eggs in the 31 Room, Barry had always found something that captured people's imagination;

something that made them amused. Sacha had been right that evening on the beach; the Bistro had the opportunity to be the fun, friendly, beating heart of Modbury. This altar would itself be the heart of the Bistro.

If only she could always be there to enjoy it.

As I sank into my seat in the stationary van, the bitter truth of her situation hit me afresh. My beautiful daughter was not indestructible, however much she had made me believe she was. We must face the reality that she would be gone soon. This had been confirmed by a recent visit to the Derriford hospital in Plymouth, after I'd found Sacha lying unconscious on the floor.

After a panicked ride in the ambulance, she'd come round in the hospital bed and clutched my hand. "What happened?" she asked.

"You blacked out," I said. "The doctors want to do scans."

A day later Sacha was able to get up. Once again, we were shown into a consultant's office, with the inevitable back-lit images of the inside of Sacha's head on the wall. The consultant might have been different – this one was a kindly-looking middle-aged woman – but the swirly grey images looked just as obscure to me.

"I have to tell you that the prognosis is not good," she said, pointing to a few of the swirly bits. "The tumours are too advanced, which is what caused the blackout." She shook her head. "We'll keep you in a few days for observation and some more tests, but I have no doubt what we'll find. I'm so sorry."

There was a silence. Then Sacha asked the question we were all thinking. "How long do I have?"

"With care, a few months."

A few months!

Suddenly I was back in the original silver-haired consultant's room at the John Radcliffe. He'd said, "Many people with low-grade astrocytomas live long lives." Only he hadn't said *how* long. Sacha had taken it to mean she'd get to old age – but maybe for him, as an oncologist, a 'long life' was anything over five years. Or even ten – and Sacha had breezed past both milestones with ease. Now, after all these years, her time had run out. Here was the finality I'd always feared but tried so hard to put to the back of my mind.

I reached for Sacha's hand and gave it a squeeze. "It's OK, Mum," she whispered. "I'll just have to enjoy the time as much as I can..."

A tow-truck slowed to a stop in front of the stricken van and Barry got out.

He came up to the window. "You all right, Annabelle?" he asked. "You look like you've been crying."

The next few months seemed to go quickly. Too, too quickly. Barry and I tried our best to open, then run the Bistro as the genial hosts, with me as 'Front of House' and Barry in the kitchen. Initially we could only offer alcohol with food as part of a meal, as we didn't have a full licence. Apparently, there were objections by other local hostelries, and it took all Barry's charm and preparation to get the justices to grant us a full licence so we could run the bar separately from the restaurant.

The altar became well established as the bar, and we added a long, upholstered bench from a Victorian station waiting room that also became a talking point. At least it was – marginally – more comfortable than the pews would have been.

At first, Sacha was still able to get up and function and would love nothing more than to get dressed and come down to the bar, greeting guests and serving drinks. But she would tire quickly, and would have to go back up to bed, where she would stay for the next couple of days. Eventually I banned her from coming down.

After that her health deteriorated to the point that she could hardly get out of bed at all, and we were offered a place in the St Luke's hospice, Plymouth. She wasn't sure initially if she wanted to go into a hospice or die at home, but we persuaded her it would be best if she was properly looked after, and that we would come and visit every day.

Barry and I carried on in the Bistro, but it was the thought of the young woman in her bed at the hospice that was on our minds all the time. Every morning one or other of us – or often both – would drive over to visit her, and would sit with her, holding her hand, stroking her cheek, talking to her – even though there were times when we had no idea if she could really hear us.

"The altar bar has been such a success," I told her one time. "It's a great talking point, especially since Wayne has made us a beautiful wooden screen to go above it..."

Or another time, "We've been so busy, we've had to take on staff. We've got a couple of local kids; one helps me with serving and the other helps your dad in the kitchen. They're good kids, too. Eager and willing to learn."

Then there was the time when I said, "You wanted us to be the heart and soul of the town. Well, you were right. I would say we are now. There's a bunch of local regulars who come in a few nights a week, and they've called themselves the Bistro Gang. Fiona, Graham and all the rest. They ask after you, and I tell them that you're doing OK..."

That was the time she opened her eyes, and whispered, "I'm so pleased it's working out, Mum... You and Dad... You deserve a bit of fun."

That was too much for me. "Oh Sacha," I cried. "I don't want fun! I want you. I want you to be better. I want you to be with me like you have been all along!"

"Sorry, Mum," she replied. "I would if I could, believe me."

A few days later I gasped in shock when I went into her room. Sacha was in bed as usual, but now her skin was paper white. With dread making me almost physically sick, I rushed over and felt her wrist. There was a faint pulse, but it was weak and irregular.

I screamed for Barry, who had been behind me on the stairs. A nurse must have come in, but I wasn't really aware. All I was focused on was the girl in the bed. I leaned over her, pushing her hair off her face, stroking her cheek. "Don't go, my love," I whispered. "Stay with me..."

There was the squeak of a shoe and Barry was beside me.

"She's still breathing..." he whispered.

But even that was going. I couldn't speak, as my throat tightened up.

Her breaths were becoming shallower and shallower...

I stroked her cheek, whispering her name. My daughter's name.

I carried on stroking Sacha's cheek, long after she had gone.

Sacha Abigail Gregory

14 July 1968 to 18 March 2000.

Chapter Thirty

Becoming Reconciled With Mother

No mother should ever have to bury her daughter.

We had the funeral on a grey, windy afternoon early in the year 2000. As Barry, Marcus, Wayne and I stood at the graveside in the churchyard of St George's, Modbury, I couldn't help but think how wrong it was that we were starting a new millennium – a new beginning – but without my beautiful daughter.

The church had been packed for the service; many of our friends from Oxfordshire had made the trip down to Devon, as had Helga and Tony from Goldhurst Terrace.

My mother came down with Ingrid, standing in uncharacteristic silence. When it was her turn to throw soil into the grave, she peeled off a glove, took a handful and threw it in. Then she looked up, and our eyes met.

Looking back, I see that moment as if I had painted it as a picture; the mourners standing in the background like statues against the grey sky; the black maw of the grave before me. On the other side, staring across at me was the small, elderly figure of my mother.

Grief had changed her.

Her face now seemed empty of judgment, devoid of all the disappointment in the choices I had made throughout my life. It all seemed to have vanished. In that instant, the woman who had withheld her approval like a precious commodity, was simply a grandmother losing a beloved grandchild. Her grief was so naked, so raw, that my defences crumbled. Here, finally, was the tenderness Mother was actually capable of. In this terrible moment, there was none of her dominance. We were equals in our grief.

I gave her the tiniest nod, and she did the same back.

A lifetime of water flowed away under the bridge.

The Bistro Gang and other friends we'd made in the first year of running Bistro 35 came in force. They might not have seen Sacha very much, and only in the bar for short periods, but they had taken her to their hearts, and their determination to show up for her meant so much to us.

After the funeral, we went back to the Bistro, where Barry had made tray after tray of buffet food, and I served everyone with drinks. The atmosphere was understandably sombre; people talking in hushed tones, and everyone coming up to me, Barry and the boys to offer their condolences.

I was standing behind the bar, thanking everyone and serving the drinks, when I became aware there was someone standing beside me. I took a sip of my drink to steady myself. It was a stone-cold certainty I was not alone, even though I knew I was the only one who'd gone behind the bar. You know the feeling, when you're sure you're being watched. You're scared to turn and look, in case you really are being observed. But then, you're also scared, in case the truth is that there is no-one.

I felt her brush against me.

"It's alright, Mum," she whispered in my ear. "I'm at peace now. No more funnies."

I couldn't think what to say.

"Nice turnout," she continued. "Must be a comfort for you." Then she added, "Although everyone looks so sad. Why's that? Why not a celebration? I had a good life. Lots of fun. Riding horses. Holidays in Alderney. Even silly things, like when I fooled my friends I could play the piano when it was actually a mechanical pianola. Or when we painted that floor in Deddington."

"You were only thirty-one," I breathed.

"But they were good years."

"You were fighting the tumours for half of them."

"But Mum, I never thought they'd kill me. Truly. Not until the end. That's what kept me going..."

Someone came up to the bar; I forget who. "Annabelle, I'm so sorry. It's so sad..."

I made all the right noises, served them a drink and they wandered off.

"Mum?"

"Yes?"

"Please don't be sad. I've said, I want you and Dad to enjoy yourselves after all you've done. The Bistro is such a success, and you've got so many lovely friends. You're doing lots of painting and exhibiting. You've got so much to celebrate. To enjoy."

"But..." I began, then stopped. How could I possibly do that when she'd gone?

"No Mum, I mean it. Enjoy yourself. Have fun in the Bistro. Be the life and soul. You deserve it."

"It's not that easy..."

"Nothing's going to bring me back. You need to be thankful for what you had. Not what you've lost."

I took a breath. "You were the best daughter any mother could wish for."

"And you were the best mum, too." I felt her lips brush across my cheek. "That's the truth. Now go out there, have fun, and honour what we had by living your own life to the full."

"You mean it?"

"I absolutely do. Bye, Mum."

"Wait! Don't go!"

"I must, Mum. But I'll always be with you. In the rustle of the wind through the trees. In the warmth of a sunset. In the beautiful song of a bird. Look for me in those."

I turned and looked.

There was no-one there.

'St Ives Harbour'

Oil on canvas 76cm x 120cm.

I discovered St Ives fairly late in life, but have constantly been drawn to the home of art in the South West.

Chapter Thirty-One

Becoming A St Ives Artist

Barry and I threw ourselves into running the Bistro. We were determined to make it 'the place to be' in Modbury – and that's what it became. Every night was a party; the bar buzzing with people having a drink before dinner, after dinner, or – once we had the full licence – just dropping in for a quick drink and a chat. They might even get some advice from our resident life-coach, Graham. I also became something of an agony aunt myself, standing behind the bar and letting people pour out their problems, while I nodded, listened and sympathised.

We had themed nights, too. Like the French cinema evenings, which in turn, led to regular winter 'Film Nights', when we would show old movies and pair each one with a suitably themed meal. One I remember was the film *Waking Ned*, served with the appropriate Guinness and Irish stew.

We tried a 'Bangers and Mash Night' on a Wednesday, and it was such a success it was soon instituted as a permanent fixture. There were regulars who would come in on the same evening each week – with such predictability that who was in the bar became a way to tell what night it was.

We employed a succession of local kids; undergrads on university holidays, A-Level students wanting to earn a few pounds in the evenings, unemployed youngsters who would come in for paid work experience. Often there was a family connection; Emily, for instance came to work with us after her brother recommended her. They would be rewarded with good pay and occasionally a free painting or collage that caught their eye.

But more than anything, they seemed to count their time at the Bistro as the time they grew in maturity and confidence. Barry and I became surrogate grandparents to these young people, and we gave them as much responsibility as we thought they could handle.

One lad, Rob, asked if he could have his nineteenth birthday party in the Bistro.

"How many people will you be having?" I asked, when he floated the idea.

"Oh, thirty. Forty max," he assured me.

In the event, over seventy showed up. We closed the Bistro for 'a private function' and found ourselves serving food to all his hungry friends, as well as helping them to slake their considerable thirst at the bar.

Rob's grandma, Joan, came. She sat up at the altar for the whole party – and as a regular, it was just like she did so many other evenings.

I offered her a drink at the start and got the standard reply, "Just the one, then..." Which is what she said before each of the many drinks she had throughout, although she never seemed any the worse for the amount of alcohol she consumed – that night or any night.

After the event finally came to an end, Barry and I were left on our own contemplating an almighty mess, caused mainly because all our current staff were enjoying themselves as partygoers rather than employees.

"We'll clear up in the morning," I muttered, and Barry agreed.

The following morning, the mess looked even worse in the daylight. We had just started to shift plates out of the bar and restaurant, when there was a knock at the door.

It was Rob's parents, Lesley and Tony, looking suitably sheepish as they crept in.

"Oh gosh, Annabelle," Lesley said, as she surveyed the wreckage. "We'd better help clear this up."

I simply nodded and stood back, ending up as the director of operations while she and Rob's dad shifted plates, washed up, cleaned glasses and filled several bin bags with rubbish.

※

Work in the Bistro was tiring, relentless and – for all the fun – took its toll on our health. Barry had had a heart bypass operation a few years before in Oxford and was supposed to be taking life easier. Not that he did, of course. For a man in his sixties he was showing no sign of slowing up and would put on his chef's whites every day and get stuck into the cooking; shouting orders at the waiting staff, chopping vegetables, mashing potatoes and plating up. All of this was always done with a glass of wine to hand – another way he was ignoring his doctor's orders.

It was one evening a couple of years after Sacha had passed away. We were doing a last clean up after the staff had left when I noticed Barry was looking a little red in the face. "Sit down, Barry love," I suggested, and poured him a glass of water. "You've been working so hard in that kitchen. You need a break. Let's close up, take a week off, and relax."

He sipped the water, and I could virtually see the cogs going round as he thought it through. "I suppose so," he admitted. "It's been pretty full on lately, and we can afford a short break." He looked up. "Alderney, I assume?"

I considered the options. Did I really want to go to Alderney? There was a time when the immediate answer would have been "yes" – but now I wasn't so sure...

It had so many family memories...

I'd first gone with Miss Palmer's Junior Naturalist Club in the 1950s, then again with her Field Observers Club a couple of years later. I had totally fallen in love with the island. So it had seemed natural to bring Barry and the children there for holidays as well, and they quickly came to love it as much as I did.

Particularly Sacha – it had always been her happy place.

I remembered her being there, even as a tiny baby. I used to love walking her pram along the coast path, with the sea crashing at the foot of the cliffs to one side, while the green fields and trees stretched away on the other. She would look up at me with those beautiful baby blue eyes and put her tiny little hand out of her blankets as if to wave at me, and I would stop, lean down and put my finger out for her to grasp in a surprisingly firm grip. Then we would walk on back to the holiday cottage and enjoy the warmth of the open fire.

As she grew up over the years, Alderney was a regular part of her life. Another memory was of her three-year-old delight at seeing cows ambling across the grass runway as we came in to land – while Barry and I were holding our armrests with white knuckles as the pilot weaved left and right to avoid them. Thankfully he had managed to land without incident.

For her and the boys, Alderney *was* their summer; the place where they spent every August (apart from the dreadful trip up to Cumbria – but the less said about that the better). They would explore Fort Clonque, Fort Tourgis and Fort Albert; Marcus marching off with the other two trotting behind as they set out to explore, as if he was Peter in the Narnia stories or Julian from the *Famous Five*.

We would relax together on the beach at Longis Bay, sitting on a blanket as the wind blew sand into our pork pies and lemonade, before Wayne and Marcus would go dinghy sailing with other children. Sacha, meanwhile, would demand I took her to the riding stables as often as possible.

Barry would come and go as the business allowed, sometimes for two or three short stays while we were on the island for the summer. I never challenged him on what he might have been up to at home; I had made it clear that although he had hurt me deeply, we had moved on, and I finally had decided to trust him. It was an unspoken agreement that he would repay that trust, and I didn't want to 'rock the boat' by openly challenging him.

Alderney was also the place where I learned to drive. Barry had discovered that passing your test on Alderney was valid for the whole of the United Kingdom, but as there were very few roads – and they were mostly in the countryside – it was much easier to take the test there than in the middle of London.

I only needed a few lessons on the country roads before the instructor decided I was ready for the test. A few days later, I was waiting in the instructor's Mini outside the airport (the start and finish point of the tests), for the examiner to arrive.

Eventually a car pulled up, and a man got out. He was middle-aged, balding, and wearing a sheepskin coat. "Right," he said, sliding into the passenger seat and checking his clipboard. "Mrs Gregory?" I nodded, my mouth too dry for talking. "Good." He gave a small burp. "'Scuse me. I've just had lunch with a charming chap. Charming." He gave me a slightly bleary-eyed look. "A Mister Barry Gregory. Offered to take me out for a meal." He looked down at his clipboard. "Oh. That's a coincidence. Gregory. Same name as you. Nice chap. Really knows his wines. Right. Pull away and turn right at the junction."

Needless to say, I passed.

Thanks, Barry.

Alderney was also, for me, a source of natural beauty that demanded to be captured in a painting or drawing. While Sacha was riding and the boys sailing, or when they had all trooped off to explore some ruin or other, I would get out my easel, pad and paints, and settle in front of one of the island's many spectacular views, happy to lose myself for hours. I think

I have now sold most, if not all, of the artworks produced there, but keeping them was never the point, it was more about the time spent painting. The composition. The light and shade. The peace and quiet. The absorption as I worked.

Sometimes Sacha would stay with me. She would sit with a book while I painted, and come over to look critically at the image. Then she would study the landscape. Even though she knew I tend towards naïve art, she would often comment on the work.

"That's nice," she would say. "It doesn't look anything like the view, but it's very nice."

Or, "The perspective's all wrong."

"It's my thing, darling. That's how I see it."

"Hmm." Then a cheeky smile. "When did you last have your eyes checked, Mum?"

Barry's voice dragged me back to Bistro 35 in the 2000s.

"Alderney?" he repeated.

"No," I said slowly. "No. I don't want to go back to Alderney any more. Too many memories."

∽∾

We decided to go to the Isles of Scilly and settled on the little village of New Grimsby on Tresco.

"There's a helicopter that goes from Penzance," Barry told me a few days later. "And there's a place in the village called the New Inn, where we can stay. There's a large lake right in the middle of the island, and there are walks all round. There's even a seventeenth century fortress called Cromwell's Castle. Apparently, you can climb up inside and look out from the top, and the views across the Atlantic are amazing." He paused. "Take your paints; you'll have a great time."

The helicopter ride got the holiday off to a great start. Barry and I did the 'crouching down' walk to the aircraft as if we were stars of some Hollywood movie, even though the rotors were at least six foot above our heads. Then there was the take-off. This was amazing; one moment we were on the ground, then there was a roar as the engine speeded up, and we lifted slowly into the air like a giant dragonfly rising from a leaf.

Almost immediately, we flew over St Michael's Mount. I was glued to the window, taking in every detail. I was so used to seeing it from the land, where it seems like a triangular cone, but of course, when you view it from the air, you can see its true shape. It's an elongated flat-topped circle, with the castle rising from the trees in the middle and the two arms of the harbour extending out – like a pair of crab's claws gathering in the small fleet of boats moored inside.

Once we were past the mount and out over the open sea, I sat back and tried to relax. This was the first opportunity to step away from the Bistro and take a breath. Ever since Sacha had passed away, I had tried to live up to her expectation and make it what she had envisaged that evening on the beach: the beating heart of Modbury. But with that came a lot of work and a fair bit of stress, especially for my husband in the kitchen.

"Barry?" I asked.

"Hmm?"

"You've been working really hard in the Bistro. Maybe you should slow down a bit. Take on someone who can help you with the cooking. A person with more experience than all these kids."

He shifted in his seat and looked over at me. "Take on a chef, you mean?"

I shrugged. "Maybe. Even if it's for a couple of nights a week, so you can have some time off."

He sat back. "I don't think so, Annabelle," he said. "I don't think I'd like that."

We had a lovely week on Tresco; the New Inn was very comfortable, and the food was good, while the landscape was varied and enjoyable to paint. But, like any holiday, it was over all too quickly, and we were headed to the heliport to get back to Penzance.

There was no sign of the sleek white helicopter when we arrived in the afternoon, instead there was only a small aeroplane standing outside the building. Barry went inside to present our tickets, while I stood by the plane with the bags. It was tiny, one of those little ones with a propeller at the front and the wing over the top of the cabin which only looked big enough for four people. Barry came out, with a concerned frown.

"There's a delay," he said. "The helicopter's having some work done in Penzance and won't be here for a few hours. We'll have to wait."

Two hours later, after we'd been sitting in the building with nothing more to sustain us than a vending machine selling fizzy drinks and chocolates, we'd had enough.

Barry marched up to the desk and demanded to know when we were going to get our flight.

"The helicopter is still a few hours from being ready to fly, sir," the girl at the desk said.

"We're not waiting any longer," Barry snapped.

"I'll see what I can do." She disappeared through a door.

A few minutes later it opened again, and a young boy in a short-sleeved white shirt and a dark tie came out of the building. He came up to us. "Mr and Mrs Gregory?"

Barry nodded. "Yes."

"My name's Tom. I'll be taking you back in the plane. If you'd follow me, please."

As Barry and I stared at each other, he marched past us and out into the evening dusk.

"But..." I began. Barry nudged me quiet.

"He must be older than he looks," he hissed.

"He looks twelve," I replied.

"They wouldn't have him if he didn't know what he's doing."

"I hope you're right."

In the event, Tom – who was probably really in his twenties – was a perfectly good pilot, and got us to Penzance without incident. Although I was rather disconcerted by the thinness of the metal fuselage beside my seat. When I pushed it with my finger, it moved in and out like a sardine can. Goodness knows if I had pushed any harder it might have given way completely, and my finger would have been waggling out in the open air.

By the time we landed it was getting late. "I don't want to drive home now," Barry said, as Tom taxied towards the terminal. "We need to find somewhere to sleep."

"St Ives is nice," Tom said. "Have you ever been there?"

I said that we hadn't.

"Try the Pedn Olva. You can usually get a room, especially as it's the end of the season. It's at the far end of the Porthminster beach, quite close to the Barbara Hepworth Museum and the Tate Gallery"

"Barbara Hepworth?" I exclaimed. "Tate Gallery?" I knew of St Ives of course, and had heard that it was something of an artists' colony, but hadn't had the time, and to be honest the inclination, to explore any further. It looked like I might have been missing out.

"Oh yes," Tom continued. "St Ives has long been the centre for arts in the South West. Apparently it all started because of the quality of the light."

We arrived at the Pedn Olva at around 10 p.m. and got a room for the night at £50. After breakfast the following morning, we walked around St Ives.

I knew, as we went into gallery after gallery along the harbour front, as we explored the sweeping curves and white walls of the Tate, as we gazed in hushed wonder at the Hepworth sculptures in the Trewyn Studio and garden...

I knew then, with absolute certainty, that I had finally found my spiritual home.

Cauliflower

Collage. 60cm x 50cm.

I have always been fascinated by everyday subjects and often see beauty in things others see as ordinary.

Chapter Thirty-Two

Becoming A Widow

The next twelve years passed in a haze of hard work, fun and frenetic activity. The Bistro was an all-consuming part of our lives; but every now and then, when I had to get a break, I would scurry down to St Ives and spend a couple of days there. I would look round the galleries for inspiration, spend time with fellow naïve artists like Judy Joel, and even submit my own works into exhibitions. Gradually, I was increasing my presence in the art scene of the South West, with my works being hung in galleries in places such as Mousehole, Penzance, Newlyn, and of course, St Ives itself.

Meanwhile, I had been accepted as a member of institutions like the Society of Women Artists and the Association of British Naïve Artists.

"After a lifetime of art, you've really made your mark," Barry said to me one day, as we were hanging a new still life of mine in the restaurant. "It's the one thing that's been a constant throughout all your years. Whether you've been a dealer in antique lace and textiles, a model, a mother or a bistro owner, you've always been an artist first and foremost."

I finished hanging the picture and stood back. "I've never told you this before," I said, then straightened the picture a fraction. "But as a small girl I made myself a promise."

"Oh yes?"

"I promised myself I would always seek out beauty in the world. As an artist, that's what I have always been striving to do."

"I see." He was silent a moment, and I could see him thinking it through. Was he wondering if I had found beauty in him? In our marriage? After all, we'd stayed together as husband and wife for fifty-three years, through his affair with the cloggy Dutch woman, the death of our daughter, the raising of two sons who'd gone on to make their own way in the world, several house moves and a number of businesses. But of course, it was not about him. It had always been about me, and my own personal search.

"And have you found it?" he asked.

I gave a small chuckle. "Does one ever? It's a constant quest; one I will be doing till the day I breathe my last." I pointed at the picture. "I've done several still-life cauliflowers like that one. And lots of beetroots as well. They might just be vegetables to you, but to me there's real beauty in them. Something in the shape. The colour." I pointed at the picture. "No cauliflower is the same. Each one is made up of hundreds of florets, and they're all completely individual." I looked back at him. "Isn't that a form of beauty?"

"He laughed. "Annabelle Gregory. Only you could find beauty in a cauliflower!"

He pulled me into his arms, drew me to him and I rested my head on his chest, listening to the flutter of his old heart. I pulled back and looked up at him. His face was one I knew as well as my own. Was the boy with the floppy hair I'd first met at the Regent Street Poly still in there? The boy I'd fallen for that night? Maybe somewhere, just without the hair and the flat stomach. I rested my head back on his chest, and he gave it a kiss.

A few days later, he was gone.

Apparently it was a massive heart attack.

All those years of stress in the kitchens, the constant glasses of wine, and the refusal to follow doctors' orders and slow down, meant that at just seventy-four, his heart had finally given up.

There was an outpouring of grief from everyone in the town, not just the Bistro Gang. As I mentioned earlier in this memoir, I opened the Bistro that night – because I couldn't think of a good reason why I shouldn't. Everyone came in – even people I had never seen in there before – and they all wanted to express their condolences. A number of the kids we'd had working there came in, many of whom were now adults with kids of their own. They wanted to say how much they'd appreciated him teaching them, not just about catering, but about life.

My heart swelled with pride in what he'd achieved, just as it was breaking over his parting.

Over the next few days, the conversation turned to the funeral – and particularly the timing. The consensus was that we should have the funeral in the evening, as Barry had been such a nocturnal person. So it was arranged for 8 p.m. a few days later.

On the stroke of 8 p.m., the procession set off up the High Street, making its slow way to St George's, where I had secured the plot next to Sacha.

Marcus, Wayne, and Barry's brother, Clive, were with me in the car behind the hearse, while a number of the Modbury townsfolk and Bistro Gang members either walked or drove behind. Ingrid had Mother, who was now very frail and becoming more and more confused, in her car.

The procession stopped anything from getting through the town, which I learned later caused bitter complaints from the tourists and non-residents who had no idea who Barry was, and why they should be so massively inconvenienced by his passing. I couldn't help thinking he'd have been very amused by this.

I'd arranged to have a line of glass jam jars with tealight candles burning inside placed either side of the path from the church door to the burial plot, as I didn't want anyone to get lost once it got dark. They gave an almost cheery feel to the event as they twinkled merrily, as if a fitting reminder of Barry's irreverent humour.

The church was packed for the service, with every pew tightly filled and people standing at the back. The Reverend Neil Barker gave a moving eulogy, which pleased me, as Barry wasn't particularly a regular churchgoer. After some hymns and readings, we all followed the coffin down the tealight path to the plot.

By the time we got there, the sun was getting low in the early summer sky, giving the graveyard a red glow as it set behind the trees. I glanced at Sacha's grave beside us. She would have been forty-six this year. I checked that the grave was well-tended, and my most recent bunch of flowers was still there, then turned back to the current funeral.

The pallbearers had organised themselves with their ropes and were lowering the coffin into the grave.

Everyone bowed their heads in silence.

The only sound was the wind blowing gently through the tops of the trees, which were silhouetted against the deep red of the setting sun. Somewhere, a single bird started singing a beautiful, melodic song.

I felt a warm glow, despite the sombreness of the situation.

"I'll always be with you. In the rustle of the wind through the trees. In the warmth of a sunset. In the song of a bird. Look for me in those."

Sacha was there.

Barry's daughter was welcoming him to her side.

'Life drawing'

Soluble oil bars on calico.

A new medium for a new phase of my life. I have discovered the joy of creating life drawings on cloth – which brings out the colours and tones in a way that paper cannot.

Chapter Thirty-Three

And finally – Becoming Annabelle Gregory

I ran the Bistro on my own for another seven years. It was the Covid pandemic – and my eightieth birthday right in the middle of lockdown – that made me decide the time had come to follow in the footsteps of old Mrs Mullery and sell up myself.

Even after the difficulties of lockdown – takeaway bangers and mash, anyone? – it was a tough decision to end it.

I discussed my thoughts one evening in the bar with Fiona, one of the Bistro Gang.

"It's been the centre of my life for twenty-two years," I said, swilling wine around my glass and staring into its depths. "I've made so many lifelong friends through it; people like you, Graham and all the other regulars. I know it's going to be hard, but I don't think I can keep it up for much longer at my age. Since Barry died, I've come to realise just how much he did."

"What will you do?" Fiona asked, ever practical.

"Painting, collage, life drawing," I replied. "There's so much that will keep me going."

"I certainly can't imagine you slowing down completely," she said.

"I've got works in two exhibitions at the moment," I told her. "And opportunities for several others. And I want to spend more time in St Ives. The Pedn Olva has become almost a second home."

"We'll all miss the Bistro," Fiona said, staring into the depths of her own glass.

"Maybe someone will take it on and keep it going," I suggested. "I'll be selling it as a going concern."

She looked up. "It wouldn't be the same." Holding my eye, she started humming a tune. I laughed; that tune had a special meaning for all of us at Bistro 35. One of our regulars, Mike Marchant, had written lyrics to it, and we'd often sung the song out in the back yard on a summer's evening, to accompaniment on the guitar. He'd called it 'Annabelle's Abattoir', as apparently the back yard was the site of an old abattoir from many years before.

You can come just as you are to Annabelle's abattoir
You can walk or drive your car to Annabelle's abattoir
You can dress scruffy, you can dress smart
Come as a duchess, a tramp or a tart,
Just as long as you look the part – at Annabelle's abattoir

People come from near and far to Annabelle's abattoir
You can bring your Ma and Pa to Annabelle's abattoir
You'll meet people that you like...
Let's just hope there's no covid spike
At Annabelle's abattoir.

You can come just as you are to Annabelle's abattoir
Lots of artwork to admire at Annabelle's abattoir
The toilet décor is a lot of fun – there's something on the wall for everyone
I often pretend that I have the runs
At Annabelle's abattoir
At Annabelle's abattoir.

Lyric extract by kind permission © Mike Marchant.

Since Barry's funeral, Mother – then in her nineties – had been going downhill fast. Once it was clear she couldn't look after herself, Ingrid organised a place in a local nursing home. She also managed the sale of Mother's house in Banbury.

It was at one of my visits that Ingrid broke the news I had long suspected. Dementia.

We were in her sitting room, having a cup of tea before going to the nursing home.

"The staff noticed it first," she said, her voice carefully measured. "Little indications. Such as Mother asking the same questions over and over. And getting confused about everyday things." Ingrid took a sip of her tea and leaned forward. "One time she even asked the staff what she was supposed to do with a plate of food when it was put in front of her."

I winced. Whatever my past relationship with my mother, it was painful to hear she was no longer able to function. She'd always been such a proud, independent woman; one who had raised three girls – admittedly in her own way – and had a great career in fashion and couture. Whatever the rights and wrongs of how she'd treated me, to end her life like this was definitely not fair.

Once again, I saw her eyes as they met mine over Sacha's grave. At least, after all the years, we'd had that moment of understanding. That was something.

"The staff wanted to have her properly assessed," Ingrid continued.

"When was this?"

"Three weeks ago. I didn't want to worry you until we knew for certain." Ingrid put her cup down. "The doctor arranged for her to see the specialist at the memory clinic. Then I had to take her to the John Radcliffe for scans."

"The John Radcliffe? Scans?" That was a memory that was all too painful.

"CT scan, blood tests. They were very thorough."

"How long do they think she has?"

"They're not sure. Could be months. Or a year or two. But she'll need round the clock care in the dementia unit. They've worked out a plan."

We went to see her that afternoon. Even though Ingrid had prepared me, it was still a shock to see her. She was in bed in her private room; a small, frail old woman, her short grey hair uncombed and her face devoid of make-up – something I didn't think I'd ever seen before.

"Hello," she said with a smile, and for a moment I thought the diagnosis was completely wrong. But then she frowned, and asked, "Are you the nurse who brings my tea?"

I went to see her a few more times, but it was clear she really had no idea who I was. Despite that, she was happy to chat away for a while, and would giggle at things I said, even though they were not meant to be funny.

That is how I finally remember her; a little old woman giving a throaty chuckle when I reminded her who I was. No longer the stern matriarch who had hung my fairy dress out of reach, or told me I couldn't stay on at St Martin's, or refused to have her grandson on her lap in case he messed up her Dior skirt. In the end, she was a just a small shell of a mother, hollowed out from the inside by that dreadful disease.

When Ingrid told me Mother had passed away, my main feeling was not one of sadness, it was one of relief.

I sold the Bistro to a young couple from Totnes, who were coffee-roasters with several café locations in the area. They renamed it The Curator and made it more of a café/tea room. I've not been in since handing over the keys, but I'm sure it's a great success, and I wish them well. They have even recently opened The Curator on the beachfront at Hope Cove.

The altar came with me to a lovely house in the grounds of a converted manor on a private estate about six miles from Modbury, where it now sits in my conservatory. This is the room that also serves as my art studio, where I spend many happy hours painting, drawing and collaging. I take regular trips down to St Ives, and have a circle of friends down there who share my passion for art in all its forms. I have a weekly life drawing class in Kingsbridge, and enjoy tea with my class mates after concentrating on creating art from the human body.

Finally, at eighty-four, I feel relaxed and content.

I have recently become mum to two kittens, Lottie and Tottie, and I am regularly visited by friends – from the Bistro, and those I have made since it was sold. Marcus and Wayne drop by occasionally, to check I am still OK, and I drive over in my old Fiat to see Ingrid and Charlotte when I can.

After all I've done in my life, I feel as if I have now answered the question set by the small girl in her rabbit costume. What is beauty?

It's having the chance to indulge in one's passions – for family, for art, for friendship.

And for life.

After all these years I have finally mastered...

The art of becoming

Annabelle Gregory

Acknowledgements

The words in this memoir are my own, but I did have help with the structure and research. Where there are some bits I didn't remember, I had help in recreating the conversations and scenes as closely as possible to what I think probably happened.

I would therefore like to say a big 'thank you' to those who have worked behind the scenes and helped me in such enormous ways – particularly Fiona and Jonathan. I appreciate Fiona's dedication and friendship, and her many hours spent interviewing me on tape – enabling me to record my memories for reference. Also to Jonathan, for his research, guidance, and many hours chasing down information. Without both of their good humour and patience, this memoir would not have been possible.

Thanks to Joel Sargent for taking the pictures of my artworks and photographs (and of me) that feature throughout this book. Thanks also to Sarah Bonner for her thorough editing of the manuscript.

Outside of the writing, I would like to make special mention of all the good-natured staff who put up with me and Barry in the Bistro. There are too many to mention individually, except that I would like to give a name-check to Rob and Emily, not just for being great members of the team, but also for their invaluable time in helping me fill in some gaps in my memory.

All profits from the sale of this book will go to The Brain Tumour Charity.

For more information, go to
www.thebraintumourcharity.org.

Published by

Winter & Drew Publishing Ltd.

winteranddrew.com

www.ingramcontent.com/pod-product-compliance
Lightning Source LLC
Chambersburg PA
CBHW061214070526
44584CB00029B/3833